108-5-UK-32

O.AY

D1225053

COMMEMORATIVE
MEDALS

BY THE SAME AUTHOR

Trade Tokens: A Social and Economic History (1971)
Agriculture, 1730–1872 (1971)
The Coming of the Railways, 1813–92 (1972)
In Preparation
Prison Reforms in Gloucestershire, 1780–1820

COMMEMORATIVE MEDALS

A Medallic History of Britain,
from Tudor times to the present day

J. R. S. WHITING

DAVID & CHARLES : NEWTON ABBOT

ISBN 0 7153 5535 X

COPYRIGHT NOTICE
© J. R. S. WHITING 1972
All rights reserved. No part of this
publication may be reproduced, stored
in a retrieval system, or transmitted,
in any form or by any means, electronic,
mechanical, photocopying, recording or
otherwise, without the prior permission
of David & Charles (Publishers) Limited

Set in 10 on 12pt Baskerville by
Avontype (Bristol) Limited
and printed in Great Britain
by Redwood Press Limited, Trowbridge & London
for David & Charles (Publishers) Limited
South Devon House   Newton Abbot   Devon

Contents

Illustrations

The medals are reproduced actual size, except for a few with a diameter over 2.25in, which have been reduced

7

The line illustrations (pages 67, 78) are from Pinkerton's *Medallic History of England to the Revolution of 1688.*

The medals were photographed by kind permission of the Trustees of the British Museum, with the exception of the M6 Motorway medal which was photographed with the permission of the Black Country Society, the *Gipsy Moth IV* medal photographed by Pinches Ltd and German air attack on London medal photographed by the Imperial War Museum.

Preface

A growing revival of interest in commemorative medals has encouraged me to write this book. The aim has been to survey the history of Britain from Tudor times to today through the eyes of the medallist. The result has been an eye-opener in many respects, for these medals have given me, as an historian, a new view of political and other events. The propaganda surrounding many incidents and personalities has become more obvious; but the pride and rejoicing in national achievements shown in many medals has been offset by the realities of treachery, murder, fear and unemployment presented by others. Warfare, transport, politics, intrigues, exhibitions, expeditions and royal occasions all have their place in the medallistic history of Britain, which highlights not only the great events but also the small. I hope this book will provide the historian or the experienced medal collector with a new light on his subject and the general reader with an introduction to the fascinating reality of history.

Another primary aim of this book is to provide the would-be collector and the museum visitor with a guide to the subject. Commemorative-medal collecting has passed from infancy to adolescence compared with trade-token collecting, which come of age, and coin-collecting, which is fully mature. What this means for anyone considering how to start a collection is considered on pp 215–16.

I have defined a commemorative medal as follows: (a) a medal struck at the time of the event which it was designed to mark (thus excluding any retrospective strikings), and (b) a medal struck for commemoration and not as a reward for merit. At times this has presented me with a fine line of definition: for example, medals struck to commemorate Arctic explorations have been excluded because they were in fact struck as rewards for those who had participated in them. Also, thousands of commemorative medals have been struck over the centuries and any survey of them must be selective. Most museums have a number of medals, but relatively few have a large store of them. It seems a pity that a greater effort is not made to maintain existing collections as new medals are struck, or to build up collections that have been haphazardly started in the past.

Chapter One

Introduction

Commemorative medals are produced to mark some notable event, and are issued for sale or general distribution. This is where they differ from the medals given by the state to individuals in recognition of military or other special services. So commemorative medals illustrate the history of a country, recording state occasions—such as coronations and marriages and deaths of public importance—and numerous other events, like victories, religious disputes and political battles. Their scope ranges from the purely parochial to the international scene and, while they record historical events, they also illustrate contemporary art. In recent years they have been struck primarily as collectors' pieces, but this is a purely modern fashion.

The production of commemorative medals can be traced back to the decadrachms given to winners in the Syracusan games, c 400 BC; and, later, to the Roman emperors of the second century AD who issued medals to distinguished visitors. In England the production of commemorative medals only began in the Tudor period, the medallic art having come via France, Germany and the Netherlands. From that time onwards their production has never ceased, much as the quantity and type of subject matter has varied.

From the producer's point of view the commemorative medal offers more opportunities than the ordinary coin, whose design tends to be restricted by the necessity of including the sovereign's bust and coat of arms. Moreover, as the medal does not have to stand up to any considerable handling, the artist is free to work in high relief, which gives him more scope with his design.

Methods of production are few and have changed only slowly over the centuries. The earliest method was that of casting and chasing; it was introduced in Italy by artists of the Renaissance period, and spread from there to the Netherlands, Germany and France in the fifteenth and sixteenth centuries, before finding its way into England. The Italians took the idea of casting medals from the casting methods they used for figures and bronze plaques, for which they were noted in the Renaissance period. They made bas-reliefs in clay or wax and then made replicas from the original moulds in bronze, the metal used for the earliest medals rather than gold or silver.

Two methods of casting could be used, the first being known as *cire perdue*, 'lost wax'. A wax model was made and painted over several times with layers of cement consisting of charcoal or fine earth stiffened with some kind of lye (a strong alkaline with detergent effect). The lye would then dry hard on the wax, and the process would be repeated as many times as was thought necessary to reach the desired thickness. When the mould was finished it was heated so that the wax inside would run out. Molten metal, gold, silver, copper or lead, was now poured into the hollow mould and allowed to set. When the metal had cooled, the mould was split open to reveal the medal. As the mould was destroyed by this process, any further medals would have to be cast from moulds made from the first medal, and, in consequence, each successive medal would become less and less sharp in its definition.

The second method started with a wax mould as in *cire perdue*, but the next step was to make sand moulds, into which the molten metal was poured. By this means the original wax mould was not destroyed, and the method was, therefore, more economic and less time-consuming. Its main disadvantage was that the sand moulds left a rough surface on the medal, which might well show some small irregularities. A finishing process was needed and this was known as flat-chasing: it necessitated the use of hammer and punches to give a better definition to the design without actually cutting into the metal. This process, also known as surface-chasing, was used for medals cast from sand moulds in gold, silver or bronze. Medals made in lead, which is softer, did not need it.

Another method of production was *repoussé* work, which began in the *cire perdue* way, a wax model being covered with lye, the wax drained out and molten metal poured in; but when the first medal had been made, instead of making moulds from it, it was used as a base on which thin plates of copper or silver were placed, being moulded to it by the use of a hammer and punches. The copper or silver plate was beaten until the image on the original medal was embossed on it. Thus *repoussé* work is done by bulging out the metal from behind, in contrast to flat-chasing, which is done from the front. The medal is finished off by flat-chasing. Clearly this was a difficult and lengthy process, but it had one great advantage, that of obtaining a high relief, which could give a striking effect to a good medal. In Germany the mould was often made of wood, though that material produced a less sharp result. *Repoussé* medals are comparatively rare because of the workmanship involved.

Engraving was another method: it differed from those previously mentioned by replacing casting by striking. There was no sudden change to this process and for a long time both casting and striking were used. If a medal was to be struck, the dies for obverse and reverse were engraved in steel, which was then chemically hardened, the required medals being made from these dies. At first this process was not very successful, as the striking was simply done by means of a hammer; but the screw-press was adopted in the sixteenth century and this improved the standard of production, though the hammer method was still used until the middle of the seventeenth-century.

Twentieth-century mechanisation has made further developments of the striking method possible. A clay model can be reproduced mechanically by electrotyping, or alternatively the clay model can be made larger than the desired medal and reduced in size by using a pantograph. Machine presses can produce the finished product at high speed, a far cry from the casting and chasing of Tudor days.

Nothing is known of the medallists who worked in the reign of Henry VIII, as none of the medals bore the artist's signature. They were cast with comparatively little skill and needed highly chasing afterwards. The medals of Edward VI's short reign show no improvement, but the reign of Mary and Philip marked a step forwards, since Jacopo da Trezzo produced medals for them in Madrid, the first signed medals in the English series. It was said of Trezzo: 'This master has no equal for portraits from life, and is an artist of the highest merit in other respects'. (See Chapter Two.)

The reign of Elizabeth I saw a great improvement in the medallic art, especially in the medals commemorating the defeat of the Spanish Armada. The medals of the reign of James I are mainly of Dutch workmanship, and few of them are signed. During his reign the new invention of the screw for striking coins and medals was coming into general use, so that medals of this period are liable to be either struck or cast. The engraved portraits of the royal family by Simon Passe are particularly noteworthy.

The reign of Charles I and the Commonwealth period abound with medals, chiefly the work of Thomas Simon, Abraham Simon, Thomas Rawlins and Nicholas Briot. Briot (see Chapter Three) invented a balance for striking coins and medals that was rejected by the Paris authorities in 1615, so he came to London, where the Mint received his invention favourably. It rendered obsolete the use of a hammer for the striking of medals. The two Simon brothers are the outstanding medallists of England. Their portrait work is expressive and accurate in its representation. Sometimes they worked together on a medal, in which case Abraham made the model and Thomas did the chasing. Thomas began work at the Royal Mint in 1636 but it is not known when his brother joined him. The work of Thomas Rawlins was well above the average, but it failed to attain the same standard of sharpness as that achieved by the two Simons. Apart from Briot, they all continued their work in the reign of Charles II, when they faced competition from the Roettier family, whom Charles had met in Holland.

Of the three brothers Roettier—John, Joseph and Philip—the eldest, John, produced the most numerous and finest works. By then, casting and chasing had been abandoned in favour of striking, with the adoption of Briot's invention. The resulting medals were very sharply cut and the portraits are expressive. The brothers' work continued throughout James II's reign, but with the coming of William and Mary the Dutch period in English medallic art began and continued until the death of Queen Anne. Among the numerous medallists of that period, Jan and Martin

Smeltzing, Jan Luder, Jan Boskam, Georg Hautsch and Jan Crocker or Croker deserve to be mentioned by name. Their style is similar to that of the Roettiers though the relief is a little lower. The reigns of William and Mary and Queen Anne have left us the most numerous and historically complete series of commemorative medals, particularly so far as the almost continual fighting of the period is recorded battle by battle. The political problems of the succession question are also reflected in medallic propaganda.

There was a marked decline in English commemorative medals when the Hanoverian kings come to the throne. Dutch medallists lost interest in English history, there were few English medallists and not many Germans came over with the Hanoverians. Workmanship and style declined and the coverage of events decreased. The medallists who deserve mention are J. A. Dassier, Richard Yeo, Thomas Pingo, C. H. Kuchler and J. G. Hancock.

Something of a revival started with the War of the Austrian Succession, 1740–48, and the Jacobite Rebellion of Bonnie Prince Charlie. The Society for the Promotion of Arts and Commerce continued the revival by issuing a series of medals to mark the events of the Seven Years' War in America and India, 1756–63. Naturally the French Revolution and Napoleonic Wars attracted the attention of medallists.

The medallic art of the nineteenth-century centres on the work of Pistrucci, an Italian who worked in England from 1815 to 1855, and the Wyon family. Pistrucci's masterpiece was the famous Waterloo Medal, but he is also known for the medals he produced for learned societies. The numerous Wyon family produced a variety of naval and military medals and a wide-ranging series of academic and other pieces. James Mudie's National Medals series also deserves mention, both English and other artists being employed on it. The nineteenth century saw a large output of medals to commemorate such structures as new town halls, churches, railways and even gasworks, as well as Sunday schools, agricultural societies, temperance societies and electioneering organisations. Many of these medals have overcrowded designs and lengthy inscriptions, but their lack of artistry is counterbalanced by their historical value.

The twentieth century has so far produced another wide range of medals, many of which have been produced primarily for collectors. Early in the century the Germans issued a range of propagandist medals to aid their war effort, among them the famous *Lusitania* medal, but apart from a few isolated commemorative instances few were struck in England or in other countries to mark particular battles or campaigns in either World War; warfare had become too grim and the acute need for metal contributed to their abandonment. The worldwide economic depression of the 1920s reduced the demand for them still further, though this did not mean that they vanished entirely. Commemorative postage stamps were cheaper to produce, and, in the realm of propaganda, the political cartoon in newspapers had become another rival to the political medal. But the last decade has seen a marked revival, ranging from gold medals which offer the purchaser an investment, to a host of cheaper medals for general public collection. The landing on the moon, the investiture of Prince Charles at Caernarvon Castle and similar popular events have been the subject of numerous medals. They have been followed by the striking of a number of sets of retrospective commemorative medals designed for collectors. Medals to mark sporting achievements have come to the fore during this century in the way that academic medals had done in the previous century.

APOLLO MOON SHOTS

The Apollo missions to the moon, though not strictly part of British history, were in a sense more than purely American events and they gave birth to a whole range of medals. The Apollo 8 mission of Borman, Lovell and Anders round the moon and back in 1968 saw the minting of a commemorative medal by Memorial Coins & Medallions Ltd, which issued 25 in platinum, 500 in gold, 500 in silver and 1,000 in bronze. The obverse shows a close-up of the moon's surface, with the earth in the far distance, showing the Americas, while circling the moon is the spacecraft; the inscription reads 'Man's first journey round the moon Christmas 1968, astronauts Borman, Lovell & Anders'. The reverse shows the spacecraft in the Pacific with an aircraft carrier nearby, with the inscription: 'Blast off 21st Dec. 1968. Splash down Pacific 27th Dec. 1968'.

The Apollo 11 mission in 1969, which made the first landing on the moon, produced a considerable range of medals. Boots the chemists arranged for Infoplan Ltd to issue a crown-size silver-plate medal designed by Turner & Simpson at 12s 6d (62½p). The obverse shows a close-up of the moon with the earth in the distance, and the space ship in flight with its flight path; the inscription reads: 'Man's first landing on the moon, 1969'. The reverse has 'Apollo 11' arranged in the centre amid three stars, and, round the perimeter, 'Neil Armstrong, Michael Collins, Edwin Aldrin'. The British Interplanetary Society presented each of the crew with 3in gold medals bearing a symbol of the earth, a space rocket and a human figure.

Investamedal Ltd commissioned Colin Phillips to design a medal, struck in platinum, gold and silver, showing Neil Armstrong's foot just touching the moon's surface, with the earth in the far background; the inscription reads: 'Armstrong sets foot on the moon, July 1969'. The reverse shows the moon in the background and from it comes the tail end of the American flag, sweeping round the atmosphere into the forefront, where it is held in the claws of an eagle. The inscription reads: 'United States of America'. Only ten of the platinum version were struck and they were offered for sale at £1,150 each. Memorial Coins & Medallions Ltd issued their medal in platinum, gold, silver and bronze, the fifty platinum medals selling at £395 each. The obverse shows the lunar module resting on the surface of the moon and is inscribed: 'Man achieves the first moon landing, July 1969'. The reverse shows the blast off with rocket and tower, and is inscribed 'Armstrong, Collins & Aldrin. Apollo 11'.

Prestons Ltd struck a silver medal with the official NASA Apollo 11 mission badge, showing an eagle alighting on the moon's surface with half of the earth visible in the background; the inscription is simply 'Apollo 11'. Its reverse shows the surface of the moon. Prestons Ltd also offered a pendant version of their medal, recalling the practice in earlier centuries of producing commemorative medals with suspension loops. Relatively few medals have portraits of the astronauts, but one such was issued by the Lombardo Mint of Vermont in silver and bronze. On the obverse the heads of the three astronauts are shown encircled with their names, while in the centre is inscribed 'Apollo XI'; in the bottom centre is the rocket just blasting off from its tower, and at either side of the top are two US flags and the two sections of the upper part of the rocket. The date of the mission is given: 'July 16–24, 1969'. On the reverse, the earth can be seen in the distance with the rocket approaching the moon, while in the foreground the module is seen on the moon's surface, in front of it the two astronauts who landed there, saluting the stars-and-stripes which they have erected nearby; in the atmosphere above is the inscription 'One small step for man, one giant leap for mankind', while below are the words 'Men on the moon. July 20 1969'.

From this selection of the large range of medals struck for the Apollo 11 mission it will be seen that most of them concentrated on the rocket or module rather than on portraits of the astronauts, and symbolism is exceptional. One feature of some medals issued was the use of hand-dried enamel to bring out the colours of the stars-and-stripes.

The Apollo 12 mission of November 1969 produced its medals, though not so many. Both the Lombardo Mint of Vermont and Memorial Coins & Medallions Ltd issued medals in silver and bronze with the same obverse—a side of the moon round which a fully-rigged sailing ship is gliding. Lombardo's medal has the date in the sky, 'Nov. 19–20. 1969', and round the perimeter, 'Apollo XII Return to the moon'. The other medal is inscribed: 'Apollo XII. Conrad–Gordon–Bean'. Its reverse shows the module blasting off from the moon with the inscription 'Moon exploration mission, November 1969'. The reverse of Lombardo's medal has the smiling three-quarter length portraits of the astronauts, dressed in their suits but without their helmets, while behind them is the module; their names are inscribed on them ('Conrad; Gordon; Bean').

Chapter Two

The Tudors

ROYAL OCCASIONS

The Tudor period marks the beginning of the medallic history of England, for from that time onwards medals to commemorate people and events were regularly produced. It is fitting to begin the series with reference to the Rose Badge medal, which was cast and chased in silver some time between October 1521 and January 1542. The reverse has the famous Tudor rose and below it is the inscription 'Defensor fidei' ('Defender of the faith'), the title which Pope Leo X conferred on Henry VIII in October 1521 as a reward for the book that Henry had written attacking the teaching of Luther. The obverse has the bust of the king, wearing a hat and cloak, and the inscription includes among the titles it ascribes to him that of 'Dom. Hyb' ('Lord of Ireland'); this indicates the latest date at which the medal could have been issued, as in January 1542 Henry changed the title to 'King of Ireland'. The British Museum also has a copper-gilt cast medal with the full-face portrait of Henry VIII wearing a hat with a feather and an ermine cloak, and round his neck the collar, medal and cross of St George. The portrait is taken from the well known painting by Holbein.

The only one of Henry's wives whose portrait has survived on a medal is Anne Boleyn, but the lead medal of her in the British Museum is in such poor condition that her features are a mere caricature of what they must once have been. The obverse has nearly a full-face portrait; she is wearing a coif with a veil, and the inscription reads: 'The moost happi anno 1534'. The reverse is plain. Henry and Anne had been secretly married in 1532 and

Page 24, The Tudors (I)
(1) Anne Boleyn, 1534; (2) Sir Thomas More, 1535; (3) Thomas Cromwell,
1538; (4) Henry VIII and the supremacy of the church, 1545; (5) Edward
VI's coronation, 1547.

their daughter, Elizabeth was born in the following year. The reference to 1534 as a 'moost happi anno' can only apply to the Act of Supremacy in that year appointing Henry head of the church in England and, in so doing, rejecting the papal refusal to allow the annulment of Henry's marriage with Catherine of Aragon. This meant that the marriage dispute was finally settled so far as England was concerned.

The execution of Sir Thomas More on 6 July 1535 was marked by the production of a cast and chased copper medal with his portrait on the obverse, in which he is to be seen wearing a biretta and a fur cloak, while the reverse has a cypress tree lying felled with an axe in the trunk; the Latin inscription refers to the sweet smell a cypress tree gives off when it is cut. An engraved silver medal appeared in his honour with a similar portrait and an inscription calling him a martyr. On the reverse is a portrait of St Thomas à Becket wearing his archiepiscopal robes, holding a book and cross; it is inscribed with the date of his martyrdom, 1171. The point here is that both Thomases died because their kings found it expedient to eliminate them. As a barrister More had earned about £400 a year, which would amount to some £20,000 today. As Lord Chancellor he was noted not only for his courageous opposition to the king; he was just and speedy in the law courts, refused to accept gifts from litigants, as judges usually did in those days. Learned and devout, he even wore a hair shirt and occasionally beat himself with a knotted cord. His *Utopia* visualised a society based on rationalism in which town and country planning would play an important role; there would be a six-hour working day, a secret ballot, no private property and education for all. He did not expect this to be a practical plan, however, for the England of his day.

A cast and chased silver-gilt medal was produced with the bust of Thomas Cromwell, Henry's secretary, dated 1538; the reverse has his coat of arms. The medal's style does not seem English or continental, though it must be one or the other, and it is impossible to say where it was executed. Son of a brewer who had been in trouble for the bad beer he sold, Thomas Cromwell had worked his way up, and his skill in tackling Henry's marital and religious problems was outstanding. In the dissolution of the monasteries he was ruthless. Three abbeys in particular were selected as examples to the others: each had an abbot of a different type—Colchester, a harmless babbler; Reading, a friend of the king; and Glastonbury, a saintlike character. The selection implied that no matter what kind of abbot a monastery had it was not exempt from the king's will. He made his point clear when he ordered the end of Abbot Richard Whiting of Glastonbury by giving his officials the following order: 'Item. The Abbot of Glaston to be tried at Glaston, and also to be executed there with his accomplices'; thus the abbot's death was ordered before his trial had taken place. Thomas Cromwell was himself executed in 1540, having—like so many of Henry's colleagues—outserved his usefulness.

The successful closure of the monasteries may have encouraged Henry to issue a medal in both gold and silver to stress his supremacy over the church in England, in 1545. It was probably the work of Henry Basse, who had been appointed Chief Engraver in November of the previous year. Curiously the artist chose to do a side-view portrait of the king which has emphasised the less pleasing profile of his head. The Latin inscription round the portrait translates: 'Henry the Eighth, Defender of the Faith and Supreme Head of the Church in England and Ireland under Christ'. This inscription is repeated in Hebrew and in Greek on the reverse, which suggests that the medal was issued for propaganda purposes among clergy in England and overseas.

As Henry Basse was the Chief Engraver from 1544 to 1549, he was responsible for the production of the first official coronation medal in English history, that of Edward VI, cast in gold and silver. It is disappointing, considering its place in medallic history, for it is of poor design and workmanship, though it is similar to Basse's medal commemorating Henry as head of the church. The obverse has the half-length portrait of the young king, wearing a crown and holding the orb and a sword. At the cardinal points are the royal badges—rose, portcullis, fleur-de-lis and harp—and between them in three concentric circles a Latin inscription which translates: 'Edward VI, by the grace of God, King of England, France and Ireland, Defender of the Faith and supreme head on earth of the Church of England; crowned 20 February 1546 at the age of ten years'. The reverse has the same inscription in both Hebrew and

Greek, together with the word 'Lambhith' ('Lambeth'), which was where the coronation took place. The date is calculated according to the old-style calendar in which the year began on 25 March (Lady Day) and not 1 January.

The British Museum has an unique medal, cast and chased in lead with a plain reverse, with Edward's portrait on the obverse. It shows him wearing a cap with a feather, a doublet and a chain, and was probably made in England.

The abortive attempt to secure the throne for Lady Jane Grey on the death of Edward VI was marked by the issuing of two medals that are virtually alike. They have a three-quarter length portrait of Lady Jane wearing a necklace with a pendant, and crowned. The inscription claims that she is queen by the grace of God. The reverse has a rose surmounted by a crown, and a Latin inscription which translates 'The supreme head on earth of the Church of England and Ireland'. The first medal is styled to imitate a coin of the time, while the second, which is made of pewter, is meant to be an accession medal.

The accession of Mary in 1553 marked a return to Catholicism after the abortive rising led by Sir Thomas Wyatt. Jacopo da Trezzo, an engraver, sculptor and medallist born at Milan and employed by Mary's husband, Philip of Spain, cast and chased a copper medal known as the 'Condition of England' medal about 1554. On the obverse is the half-length portrait of the queen wearing a veiled coif, an embroidered gown and a pendant pearl. The reverse shows Mary playing the part of Peace, seated and holding an olive-branch and a palm, while burning emblems of warfare; behind her is a group of suppliants, and in the distance a circular temple. The reverse presumably refers to the overthrow of Wyatt and the restoration of Catholicism.

Trezzo was responsible for the production of wedding medals for Mary and Philip, in two versions—one in copper-gilt and the other in both gold and silver. The copper-gilt version has the half-length portrait of the queen on the obverse and the half-length portrait of Philip on the reverse, dressed in armour. The gold and silver versions are smaller, showing the head and shoulders of the same portraits; they give a more balanced design, bringing out the best features of the portraits to good effect, whereas the copper-gilt

3

Page 28, The Tudors (II)
(1) Queen Mary I, 1555; (2) Mary and Darnley, 1565; (3) Lady Jane Grey, 1553; (4) and (5) Queen Elizabeth's Phoenix Badge, 1574.

version gives a poor rendering of the half-length figures, which spoil the proportions of the medal. The marriage was not popular in England in spite of the twenty cartloads of gold that Philip brought with him; the feelings of the country were expressed by the snowballs that boys threw at Philip's embassy when it arrived on New Year's Day, 1554.

No coronation medal appears to have been issued to mark Elizabeth I's coronation, but an oval Garter Badge medal, cast and chased in silver, was executed for presentation when occasion arose. On the obverse it has a portrait of the queen wearing a coronet of pearls and a dress with a large ruff. The inscription is taken from that on the Garter Badge. The reverse has the royal coat of arms supported by an angel and the same inscription. In 1572 Elizabeth recovered from an attack of smallpox which fortunately left her face unmarked, and a medal was issued to celebrate the occasion; on the obverse appears her portrait, while on the reverse is a snake fastened to St Paul's hand, which remains unharmed. Another cast and chased medal in silver is known as the Phoenix Badge, and though it bears the date 1574 it probably refers to the same attack of smallpox. The date may also stress the fact that plague was widespread in London in that year. On the obverse is a portrait of the queen wearing pearls in her hair and a dress with a high ruff, with a Latin verse in her praise encircling the portrait. On the reverse is a phoenix rising from the flames, and above it a crown, 'ER' and the roughly incised date '1574'; round the phoenix is a Latin verse flattering Elizabeth as being our phoenix in all but death. Elizabeth had adopted the phoenix as her personal badge. The medal was probably the work of a Dutch refugee, John Rutlinger, who was under-graver to the Mint.

Mary, Queen of Scots, was Queen of England according to Roman Catholics, and consequently her existence was a threat to Elizabeth. Mary's career of marriages and murders was duly recorded on numerous medals. When she married the Dauphin of France in 1558, a silver medal was issued showing the busts of Mary and Francis face to face. She is wearing a rich head-dress and a medallion hanging from a chain, while he is dressed in armour; a crown is shown above their heads, and the inscription translates

'Francis and Mary, King and Queen of Scots, Dauphin and Dauphiness of Vienne'. (Vienne was the capital of Lower Dauphiné.) The reverse shows the shield of the Dauphiné and Scotland impaled and crowned between the initials F. and M., which are each crowned; and the Latin inscription reads 'He has made both one. 1558'. A much more common medal was issued in silver and copper with the same design, slightly larger. The following year was marked by a wide-ranging issue of medals to celebrate Francis and Mary's accession to the throne of France. One of them, usually found in copper though it is known in silver as well, has an interesting obverse showing two globes between labels inscribed 'Unus non sufficit orbis' ('One world is not enough'), surmounted by a crown; round the whole is a Latin inscription, meaning: 'All things are to be measured by calculation and reason'. The reverse has a shield quartered with the arms of France and England and surmounted by a crown, the whole surrounded by the collar of the Order of St Michael. The medal was designed by Marc Bechot (1520–60), who was Engraver-General to the Mints of France.

A medal that appeared in 1560, and seems to have been issued in most metals, hinted at Mary's claim to the throne of England. On the reverse are two crowns of different sizes, one over the other, between the earth and clouds, in which appears a third crown composed of stars. The Latin inscription translates 'And waits for another. 1560'. The first two crowns are those of Scotland and France, and the one in the clouds that of England. The obverse has a shield bearing the arms of the three kingdoms. Fortunately for Elizabeth the death of Francis in the same year deprived Mary of one throne.

Mary's marriage to the Earl of Darnley in 1565 was marked by medals that are very rare today. One of them, struck in silver, has the busts of Mary and Darnley face to face and both crowned; she is wearing an embroidered bodice and has long hair, while he is dressed in armour. The reverse bears the Scottish arms between two thistles and a Latin inscription which translates 'Whom God hath joined together let no man put asunder'. Darnley was Mary's probably immoral, bad-tempered and drunken cousin; he was responsible for the murder of her friend Rizzio, but was himself murdered in 1567. Mary's long exile in England after her disastrous marriage to Bothwell was marked in France in 1579 by the striking of a medal in silver and copper. The obverse has the arms of Scotland, while the reverse has a hand from the clouds pruning a withered branch from a vine; the Latin inscription translates 'Virtue is strengthened by affliction'. The device on the reverse is based on the pattern which Mary had embroidered on a cushion ten years earlier. Mary's execution in 1587 was not marked by a medal, and it was not until the eighteenth century that one was struck.

EXPLORATION

Sir Francis Drake's voyage round the world, 1577–80, is commemorated by a very rare silver medal measuring $2\frac{3}{4}$in across. On one side it shows the eastern hemisphere and on the other side the western. A dotted line marks the course of Drake's voyage, and the medal also shows Frobisher Strait, indicating that the artist, who was probably Michael Mercator, had taken the voyages of Frobisher between 1576 and 1578 into account. Drake's voyage was one of the greatest Elizabethan sea ventures; his ships averaged 88 miles a day when the trade winds were with them and some 50–60 when they were not. He traversed the 300 mile Straits of Magellan in a record sixteen days (Magellan had taken thirty-seven, and others over forty days). After treasure-hunting up the west coast of South America (and picking thirteen bars of silver from the side of a sleeping Spaniard!) he went on to try and find the west end of the supposed North-west Passage in the area of California. In 1936 a plate was found near San Francisco that is probably the one he put up to claim the land for his queen. He continued his voyage round the world and returned home with a profit of 4,700 per cent. The delighted queen came down to knight him on the deck of the *Golden Hind*, the occasion being marked by two unexpected incidents: the queen's garter came off as she went aboard, and, being handed it back, she coolly lifted her skirts and replaced it in full view of all present; and the rush of courtiers to cross the gangplank to view the ceremony led to its collapse and a ducking for 100 of them, much to the amusement of the queen and Drake.

Page 32, The Tudors (III)
(1) and (2) Drake's world voyage, 1580; (3) and (4) Earl of Leicester and
the sheep, 1587; (5) and (6) Armada and the Pope, 1588.

WAR AND POLITICS

When Robert Dudley, Earl of Leicester, was recalled from his military and political command in the Netherlands in 1587, he arranged for a Dutch silver medal to be cast and chased to stress his protest at the treatment he had received. The obverse has a three-quarter-length portrait of the earl, wearing a cap with a feather and engraved armour, while the reverse shows a flock of sheep being deserted by their dog, with the Latin inscription 'Compelled to leave, not a flock but thankless beasts'. It is not surprising that Leicester resented the way in which he was super-seded in his command, for he had been asked to do an almost impossible task in the first place. From a political point of view he had to modify the constitution in the Netherlands and stabilise the currency, and from a military point of view he was ordered to 'bend his course to make a defensive rather than offensive war' and to avoid battles he was likely to lose. He was faced with difficult provisioning problems, finding, in fact, that some of his troops' food was reaching the enemy; and many of his men were deserting to that enemy, who gave them passes to enable them to reach nearby ports. He drew up a fifty-five clause disciplinary code to try and cope with the situation, listing regulations for every even-tuality. Rule 5 read as follows:

> And for that it often happeneth, that by permitting of many idle women in an armie, sundry disorders and horrible abuses are com-mitted: Therefore it is ordeined that no man shall carrie into the fielde, or deteine with him in the place of his garrison, any woman whatso-euer, other than such as be knowen to be his lawful wife, or such other women to tende the sicke and to serue for launders . . . upon paine of whipping and banishment.

His privates received eightpence a day, out of which their food and drink cost them $4\frac{1}{2}$d, and they had to pay for their gunpowder, which worked out at 7d for twelve shots. (The apparent employment of female nurses at that time is an interesting sidelight.)

The Spanish Armada's defeat in 1588 was the occasion for the issuing of a number of medals. In England medals were cast in gold and silver and in two different sizes with slightly differing designs. The larger has a portrait of the queen in high relief facing the viewer, wearing a crown and very high ruff, and holding the sceptre and orb; the Latin inscription is not particularly clear but it seems to suggest that the queen is the most precious treasure in all the world. On the reverse is a bay-tree on an island, the tree remaining uninjured in spite of the lightning which strikes it; the Latin inscription translates 'Dangers themselves do not touch her'. (The bay-tree was supposed to be immune to lightning, which in this case represents the Armada.) The oval medal was cast and chased with a ring for suspension, which suggests that it was given to be worn. The smaller medal is thought to be by Nicholas Hilliard, who normally painted miniatures; it is nearly round, with a ring for suspension. The obverse has a portrait of the queen resembling that on the larger medal, but she is not holding the sceptre or the orb; also, the workmanship is much finer than on the larger medal, being particularly rich in detail on the dress, ruff and hair. The reverse is similar but with the addition of the letters 'ER' in the sky above the uninhabited island. Another medal cast and chased in gold and in silver, with a suspension loop, has a portrait of the queen similar to that on the smaller of the medals previously mentioned, and on the reverse has the Ark floating in the midst of a rough sea under a shining sun, with a Latin inscription stressing that it is floating calmly in the midst of the raging sea. This may be an allusion to the English flagship, the *Ark Royal*.

Dutch medals commemorating the defeat of the Armada were mostly struck, rather than cast and chased. One such silver medal satirises the blindness of the Papacy, showing the Pope and the King of Spain, the Emperor and others sitting together in a meeting with their eyes bandaged, while spikes are springing up in the floor in their midst. The Latin quotation from the Bible translates 'It is hard to kick against the pricks'. On the reverse is a dramatic scene of the Armada being driven on the rocks—ships are sinking and bodies floating in the water. The Latin inscription is divided into two parts: 'Veni, vide, vive' ('I came, I saw, I survived'), a neat little parody of Caesar's famous comment; the other part is taken from Psalm 86, verse 10, and translates 'For Thou art great, Thou workest wonders, Thou, only Thou, art God'.

Another Dutch silver medal showed the naval engagement and the destruction of the Spanish fleet on the obverse, with the word

Yahweh written in Hebrew above. On the reverse the church is seen standing firm on a rock in the middle of a stormy sea; the Latin inscription says that the church, though dashed against, is uninjured. Other Dutch medals stress the alliance between England and Holland by showing two oxen yoked to a plough, or, alternatively, two pots tossed in a rough sea, to stress the dangers of factional differences, with inscriptions which translate 'Certain, if they crash, to break'. Others stress gratitude at the defeat of the Armada by showing a globe released from the bands that the King of Spain had fastened round it, young birds beating off a bird of prey, and so on.

Chapter Three

The Early Stuarts

ROYAL OCCASIONS

Commemorative medals of the reign of James I (1603–25) are not numerous, possibly because his succession to the throne was not disputed, apart from the Gunpowder Plot. The majority of medals are purely personal, being portraits of the king and members of the royal family. James's accession was marked by the striking of a small silver medal at the Royal Mint, with a portrait of the king in armour and a Latin inscription which, translated, reads 'James I, Emperor of the whole island of Britain and King of France and Ireland'. This was the first time that a king of England had styled himself an emperor, but such vainglory is in keeping with James's character. A man whose father had been murdered and whose mother had been executed was likely to be insecure, especially when his own disabilities, such as having a tongue too ₁rge for his mouth, are taken into account.

His silver coronation medal was designed for distribution to the people, and was the first souvenir medalet of its kind. Future coronations were to be marked in a similar way. On the obverse is a portrait of the king surrounded by a Latin inscription, which translates 'James I, Caesar Augustus of Britain, Caesar the heir of the Caesars, presents this medal'. On the reverse is a crowned lion rampant holding a beacon and wheatsheaf, and the Latin inscription translates: 'Behold the beacon and safety of the people'. It is not very easy to find this medal in good condition today.

Better portraits of the king and queen are to be found on the engraved plates done by the Dutch engraver Simon van de Passe

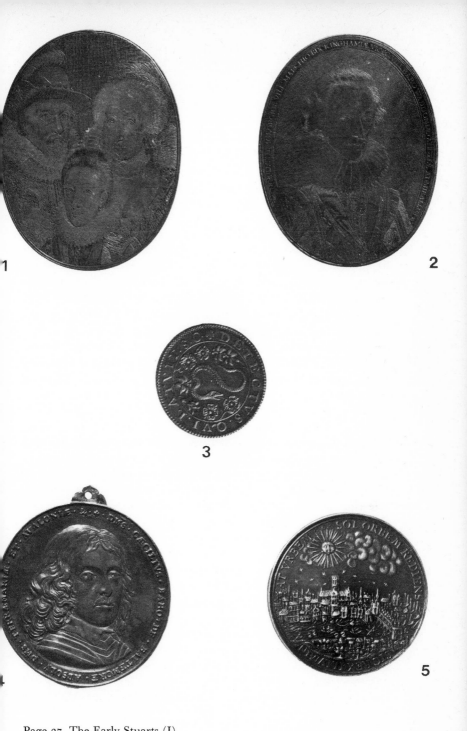

Page 37, The Early Stuarts (I)
(1) James I, his Queen and Prince Charles, 1616; (2) George Villiers, 1618;
(3) Gunpowder Plot, 1605; (4) Lord Baltimore, 1632; (5) The return of
Charles to London, 1633.

(1574–1644). Passe came to England in 1613 and stayed for ten years before going to Denmark. Strictly speaking it cannot be said that his engravings were medals, since they were just metal plates engraved by hand; nevertheless their superb workmanship entitles them to a place in this book. He did a whole series of the royal family in 1616, usually in silver, though some in gold; their detail is noteworthy and they display a rare depth of perspective. The most interesting is that depicting the royal family group, including the king, the queen and the Prince of Wales. James is wearing a typical Stuart hat with a large feather, his wife, Anne of Denmark, has a high lace collar and a low-cut dress, while the prince is hatless and dressed in a fashionable suit with a high stiff collar. On the reverse their three coats of arms are displayed amid much decoration. The diameter is 2½in. Matching plates of slightly differing sizes were done for them separately.

Two years later, in 1618, Passe did a plate of George Villiers, Marquis of Buckingham. The obverse has a three-quarter-length portrait of the marquis, who became a duke in 1623. This oval medal was struck in silver. On the reverse Passe engraved Buckingham's coat of arms. Buckingham was a brave, resourceful man who became the king's favourite; but, like most favourites, he was a political problem because he would interfere with the running of the country. He accompanied Prince Charles to Spain in disguise to court a Spanish princess; but their manners were so bad by Spanish standards that they caused a breakdown in relations with Spain, and they returned to demand a war—which the ageing king allowed them.

No English medal was struck to mark the failure of the Gunpowder Plot, and we have to turn to Holland for the only example, struck in silver the year after the Plot by order of the Dutch Senate. The obverse has a snake gliding among lilies and roses, with a Latin motto which may be translated 'Discovered in his hiding place'. The reverse has the word Yahweh written in Hebrew as the centrepiece of the sun (sometimes described as a crown of thorns and not a sun); the Hebrew and Latin inscriptions combined read 'Yahweh, who keeps James, has not slept'. To find out the date one has to take the letters which are larger than the rest ('non DorMItastI antIstes IaCobI') which give one MDCIIIII

(1605): inscriptions written in this way are known as chrono-grammatic inscriptions. The medal suggests that the Dutch were making the point that the Plot was the work of Jesuits.

The marriage of James's daughter, Elizabeth, to Frederick, Count Palatine, on 11 February 1612/13, was the occasion for the casting of a silver-gilt medal depicting Frederick on one side and Elizabeth on the other. He is dressed in armour and his bride in an embroidered gown with a high ruff. In spite of James's chronic shortage of money the wedding was lavish enough: Elizabeth's clothes cost £6,252, her jewels £3,914, and £7,680 were spent on fireworks. The expense of her journey abroad came to £13,555, and the cost of furniture for her personal room a further £3,023; on top of all this was a dowry of £40,000. The marriage was to present considerable problems for James, for in 1618 the Bohemians rose against their Hapsburg overlord and offered their throne to Frederick. When he accepted, the Hapsburg emperor, who was also his overlord, expelled him from the Palatinate, his hereditary state, and then drove him out of Bohemia. However, before this disaster, a medal had been cast and chased in German silver to commemorate Frederick's coronation as King of Bohemia in 1619. The obverse depicts Frederick and Elizabeth with a Latin inscription recording their coronation and expressing the hope that they will have a prosperous reign. The reverse bears the badge of the Garter, since Frederick had been elected a Knight in 1613, and a lion holding a sword in front of a flourishing rose-tree, below which is a serpent.

James's reign saw the issuing of two medals of interest to Oxford University. The first was an oval silver medal cast and chased to commemorate Nicholas and Dorothy Wadham; Nicholas, who founded the Oxford college named after him, died in 1609 and his wife in 1618, when the medal was struck. On the obverse is a three-quarter-length bust of Nicholas wearing a cloak, with the inscription 'When Christ who is our life shal appeare', which is concluded on the reverse with the words 'We shal appeare with Him in glory'. Dorothy is portrayed on the reverse in an embroidered gown and a hat. On both sides the border has a floral wreath united by skulls. The other medal, in lead, was struck in 1612 in honour of Sir Thomas Bodley; its obverse records in Latin his foundation of the public library at Oxford (the Bodleian) which still bears his name today, and his portrait in academic dress. The reverse has the figure of Eternity holding heads of Sun and Moon.

The reign of Charles I (1625–49) was heralded by the issue of a gold coronation medal in 1626. The obverse has the bust of the new king wearing his crown, and its Latin inscription translates: 'Charles I by the grace of God, King of Great Britain and Ireland'. The reverse has an arm brandishing a sword, with the Latin inscription 'Until peace be restored upon earth. Crowned 2 February 1626'. This inscription is unusual for a coronation medal, for it holds out the prospect of the vigorous prosecution of war against Spain, partially as an outcome of Charles's unhappy attempt to find a Spanish bride, and partially to assist the United Provinces in their fight against Spanish domination; it also refers to attempts to restore Charles's brother-in-law, Frederick, to his Bohemian throne. The medal was struck by Nicholas Briot, who had been Chief Engraver to the Paris mint until the autumn of 1625, when he fled to England to escape his debts. Ten years earlier, as recorded in the Introduction, he had invented a balance for striking coins which was a major improvement on the old method of striking by a hammer; but he had clashed with his superiors and his invention was a source of irritation to his colleagues in the trade. It was not until 1623 that his invention was accepted by the Paris mint for a trial period. He was well received in England and his invention given its due; he was told to start work on the coronation medal immediately. He was Chief Engraver from 1628 to 1633, when he returned to the Paris mint.

Briot was also responsible for the casting and chasing of a gold medal claiming Charles's dominion over the sea, in 1630. Its obverse has a portrait of the king with a particularly large ruff, and its reverse a man-of-war in full sail. It was in fact at this time that Charles issued a notice to his minister at the Hague saying, 'We hold it a principle not to be denied that the King of Great Britain is a monarch at sea and land to the full extent of his dominions'. The seventeenth century was to witness a growth in England's colonies with a consequent strengthening of her control over the seas.

An example of colonial enterprise was that of Lord Baltimore, who was responsible for founding the colony of Maryland. A cast and chased silver medal was issued to commemorate the event in 1632. On the obverse is the bust of Lord Baltimore wearing armour, while the reverse has a map of Maryland, showing Chesapeake Bay and the River Potomac; the sun is shining on the map and on Baltimore's coat of arms, which covers part of it. The Latin inscription translates 'As the sun you will enlighten America.' Maryland was the first proprietary colony, and Baltimore as its owner was virtually its king. His brother led the first expedition to the colony, taking some 300 settlers. They went out as family units, which made for a happier situation than that faced by the early Virginians, for there the first settlers had been men only, working under discipline in what turned out to be a malarial area. The Marylanders were fortunate in being able to buy an Indian village, complete with huts and crops, which they named St Mary's. This became a real home for them and enabled them to avoid the communal work and danger of starvation that the Virginians had had to cope with. Corn and tobacco became their main crops.

Briot was ordered to produce a second coronation medal to commemorate Charles's coronation in Scotland in 1633. Although Charles ruled both Scotland and England, as his father before him, two separate coronations were necessary, since the kingdoms were not united until 1707. The obverse depicts Charles wearing his crown and the reverse a thistle and rose-tree combined, with the date of the coronation (18 June 1633). Round the edge is a Latin inscription saying that Briot made the medal from Scottish gold; this was mined in Niddesdale and Clydesdale. Specimens were also struck in silver. Charles's return to London was celebrated by gold and silver medals depicting him riding a prancing horse, with a view across the Thames to St Paul's cathedral on the reverse. The sun is shining brightly over the scene, and the Latin inscription translates 'As the sun returns in orbit, so the king illuminates the city'. The St Paul's shown is the old cathedral, which was destroyed in the Great Fire of 1666; it had a tower and, until 1561, a spire on top of the tower (the spire was destroyed by fire in that year). On the medal the south end of London Bridge shows four heads on spikes on Traitor's Gate as a warning to would-be criminals.

In the centre of the bridge stood Nonsuch House, a four-storied building that had been prefabricated in Holland, shipped to England and fitted together with wooden pegs. Numerous boats can be seen on the river, which was a major thoroughfare for Londoners with its ceaseless 'taxi' service of boats.

CHARLES I AND PARLIAMENT

There are no medals recording the early contest between Charles I and Parliament until a gold one was issued in 1641 to commemorate the execution of Thomas Wentworth, Earl of Strafford. It shows him wearing armour and is in high relief. Wentworth was Charles's right-hand man, whose policy of a vigorous and unified administration was known as 'Thorough'. He became a symbol of executive government which Parliament wished to check. An impeachment or political trial of Strafford failed to result in a conviction, so the House of Commons passed a bill of attainder saying that he ought to die: judicial murder in fact. Two hundred and fifty MPs were absent when the vote was taken, 204 being for the bill and 59 against. In the Lords, one-third were absent, and the vote was 26–19 for his death. Reluctantly Charles signed the death warrant of his closest adviser and Strafford went to his death.

In 1642 when Charles left for York, Parliament raised an army under the Earl of Essex and issued a declaration that its aim was to preserve 'true Religion, Laws, Liberties and Peace of the Kingdom' while also wishing to preserve the safety of the king's person. To emphasise their point they had two different medals issued. The first one was cast and chased in silver-gilt in oval form with a loop for suspension. On the obverse is the bust of the king wearing his crown and his Knight of the Garter badge, with the inscription 'Should hear both houses of parliament for true Religion and subjects fredom stand'. The reverse has an engraving of the two Houses of Parliament, together with the king and the speaker. The second was struck in silver with a reverse similar to the first, but its obverse depicts a ship in full sail, intended to represent the ship of state. The inscription on the reverse translates 'For Religion, People and King'. The medal appears to have been struck upon a piece of cast metal and from copper dies, which are known to have existed and are considered to be matrices of a seal.

Page 43, The Early Stuarts (II)
(1) Earl of Essex, 1642; (2) Battle of Edgehill, 1642; (3) Declaration of
Parliament, 1642; (4) Earl of Strafford, 1641; (5) Bristol taken, 1643.

The opening and indecisive battle of the Civil War between king and Parliament (Royalists and Roundheads) was fought at Edgehill in 1642. The Roundheads wore orange scarves to distinguish their forces. Many stories have been recorded of incidents in the battle: for instance the king's standard bearer was cut down, but his hand was grasping the standard so firmly that a Roundhead had to chop his dead arm off to secure it; the standard was then carried away with the arm attached to it, but a certain Captain Smith rescued it and was rewarded with a knighthood. Neither side secured a military victory, but as the Roundheads withdrew in such a way as to allow the Cavaliers to advance towards London, the latter can be said to have won a strategic victory.

Two medals were issued to commemorate the event, one by each side. The oval Cavalier medal was cast and chased in silver by Thomas Rawlins, and had a suspension loop. On the obverse the king is shown dressed in Garter robes, while on the reverse he appears on horseback. Thomas Rawlins had served under Briot at the Mint, and was to show himself to be a staunch royalist for the rest of the war. The Roundheads' medal was also in an oval loop-suspension design, but cast and chased in silver-gilt. The obverse depicts the Earl of Essex on horseback with the battle raging in the distance, while the reverse has his coat of arms.

During the remaining years of the war numerous medals bearing the portraits of leading figures were to be issued by both sides. The Roundheads were first to issue theirs, beginning with one in honour of Lord Fairfax in 1643. This oval silver medal was chased and cast with a loop for suspension, and was probably intended as a military reward; the obverse has a three-quarter length bust of Fairfax in armour, and the reverse has his coat of arms. When the war started, he was appointed commander-in-chief of the Roundhead forces in the north, and the battle of Marston Moor was his greatest victory. His colleague, the Earl of Manchester, was the subject of a medal similar in shape and method of production, bearing his bust on the obverse and the two Houses of Parliament complete with the king on the reverse. Manchester was in command of the Eastern Association army, made up from Parliamentary forces from seven counties. The Earl of Essex's second in command, Sir William Waller, was the subject of a third similar medal, which, in addition to his portrait, bore the inscription 'The valiant commander Sir William Waller. Should hear both houses of parliament for true Religion and subjects fredom stand'. Like the Earl of Manchester's, its reverse bears the two Houses of Parliament. When Cromwell pressed for the removal of lukewarm commanders by the Self-denying Ordinance, Waller was removed and later fell under suspicion, being twice imprisoned. He assisted in the restoration of Charles II, and died in 1668. Completing the 'set' of medals on Roundhead leaders in the early years of the war was a gold medal issued in 1643 to honour John Hampden, who was killed at the battle of Chalgrove Field. The obverse has a portrait of Hampden in armour, while the reverse has an axe and the inscription 'Inimica Tyrannis'. Hampden had made his name in 1637 when he refused to pay his £1 ship-money tax, which Charles had revived in order to defend England from pirate attacks up the Thames and Severn and raids on Portsmouth and Plymouth. Normally it applied only to ports, in times of emergency, these then being required to supply ships or money; but Charles extended the tax to inland towns. It had a devastating effect on local towns, as can be seen from the fact that Sudbury in Suffolk had to pay £85 in 1635 when it was normally used to raising the occasional £1 to £5 for repair of the local bridge. Hampden's stand against the tax was one of the early acts of defiance against Charles's regime.

In 1643 the Cavaliers began their issue of propaganda medals with two to mark the Roundheads' surrender of Bristol. Thomas Rawlins was probably responsible for a silver medal bearing the bust of Charles on the obverse with the letters 'OX', referring to Oxford where it was struck. The reverse has a fine view of Bristol with a Latin inscription recording its capture. The second silver medal is virtually the same, except that its view of Bristol is less well executed and the letters 'OX' are omitted; it was probably the work of David Ramage. Prince Rupert, in charge of the assault, used the password 'Oxford', and made his men wear something green and bare their necks to distinguish them from their enemies.

The beheading of William Laud, Archbishop of Canterbury, on 10 January 1645 was marked by a medal cast and chased in silver. The reverse was left plain, but the obverse carried a portrait of Laud dressed in academic robes and wearing a biretta. It had

Page 46, The Early Stuarts (III)
(1) Archbishop Laud, 1645; (2) Prince Rupert, 1645; (3) Attempted release of Charles I, 1648; (4) and (5) Charles I's execution, 1649.

been Laud's policy to restore the traditional type of order and decency in Church of England services and put an end to Puritan experiments. When Dean of Gloucester Cathedral, Laud had moved the communion table to the position of the altar, an action that was used in evidence against him by the headmaster of the King's School when Parliament turned on him. Laud had also denounced the growing custom of parishioners appointing lecturers to preach the kind of sermons they liked when their vicars failed to give them satisfaction. Hundreds of Puritans emigrated to New England because of Laud (one being the Rev Samuel Whiting, an ancestor of the author, who settled in Massachusetts). Laud had been sent to the Tower when Strafford was arrested and there he stayed until his execution in 1645.

Prince Rupert, grandson of James I, was the subject of an oval silver medal, cast and chased, as a military reward. It depicts him wearing armour and holding a marshal's baton, his coat of arms being on the reverse. Prince Rupert was Charles's cavalry commander, renowned for his spectacular charges which generally took his men straight through the enemy lines to their camp. At Edgehill his men virtually abandoned the battle for plunder. Later on, when he surrendered Bristol suspiciously quickly, he had to face an enquiry, which, though it cleared him, left him in doubtful favour with the king.

The execution of Charles I in 1649 was the occasion for the issuing of a whole range of medals, most of which were made by Thomas Rawlins. One, cast and burnished in silver, has the bust of the king wearing decorated armour, with a Latin inscription declaring him to be divine and pious, on the obverse, and on the reverse a hammer splitting as it hits a diamond resting on an anvil with the word 'inexpugnabilis' ('invincible')—a reference to the king's spirit. Another depicts the king wearing the robes and star of the Garter with a crown of thorns and a scroll on which is a Latin inscription implying that, though Charles died, he lives on in a Christian sense. The reverse side of this cast and chased silver medal shows a rock buffeted by winds and waves with an inscription that translates 'triumphant and immovable'. There are a variety of these medals. Rawlins also produced some bearing the portrait of the king on one side and that of the queen on the other.

One Dutch cast and chased silver medal has a portrait of the king in armour with a Latin inscription that translates 'King Charles. What my people did to me'. The reverse had the head of Medusa surrounded by a legend in three circles, the two outer divided by a flaming sword, arms and a thunderbolt. The translation of the inscription reads 'The English assembly blaspheme God, murder the king and despise the Law'. The head of Medusa is symbolic of rebellion, sedition and anarchy. One memorial medal was struck by someone called 'F' in Germany, or possibly Holland, and it depicts Charles surrounded by a double circle of German inscription: 'Charles I, by the grace of God, King of England, Scotland and Ireland; God and the Sovereign power suffer'. The inscription is concluded with the words 'by the mob's might and strife' on the reverse, which also depicts a seven-headed monster towering over the decapitated head of the king, the crown and a sword lying nearby. The many heads of the monster are intended to illustrate the variety of evil thoughts and actions of the king's rebellious subjects. This medal was struck in silver and is fairly common.

THE COMMONWEALTH

In the same year as the king died, John Lilburne (1618–57), the Leveller leader, was tried and acquitted on a charge of high treason against the Roundhead cause. His acquittal led to the striking of a silver medal depicting him in the middle of an inscription arranged in three concentric circles: 'John Lilborne saved by the power of the Lord and the integrity of his jury who are juges of law as wel as fact, Oct. 26. 1649'. On the reverse is a rose in the centre of four concentric circles inscribed with the names of the twelve jurymen and the date of the trial.

The Leveller movement lasted some ten years, and was once wrongly thought to be a republican democratic movement. Son of a wealthy landowner, Lilburne sprang to fame in 1638 when he was punished by being lashed with a knotted whip for distributing propaganda against bishops. In 1647 he was put in the Tower of London by the remnant of the House of Lords because he had insulted one of its members. From there, in conjunction with his aide, John Wildman, he led the Leveller movement with the

Page 49, The Early Stuarts (IV)
(1) and (2) Cromwell and Fairfax—devils and fools, 1650; (3) Lilburne,
1649; (4) and (5) Battle of Dunbar, 1650.

publication of *The Case of the Army Truly Stated* and the *Agreement of the People for Peace*, which called for the abolition of monopolies, freedom of trade, codification of laws, a 'free-born' suffrage, biennial parliaments, and a redistribution of parliamentary seats, among other reforms. Fearing that Lilburne would stir up discontent in the army, Cromwell visited him in prison and offered to secure his freedom if he would not disrupt the delicate balance of relations between the Roundhead army and the Parliament at a time when negotiations with the king had to be undertaken. Lilburne refused, but Cromwell started proceedings for his release nonetheless, which led to the Levellers suggesting that Cromwell was intending to accept the bribe of an earldom from Charles I. Lilburne was released in November 1647 and continued to cause trouble for Cromwell, which led to his further arrest. In the 1650s, after his release, Lilburne tried to open negotiations with the exiled Charles II for a monarchical restoration on Leveller terms; but as he died in 1657 he never lived to see the monarchy restored. He had denounced the king's execution as premature. His acquittal medal may be compared with those issued by the late eighteenth-century radicals, Hardy, Tooke and Thelwall, on their release, for both seventeenth- and eighteenth-century medals pay their respects to the British judicial system.

Following the death of the king, the Roundheads were keen to promote their cause as best they could, and this led to the issue of a number of medals in 1650. Thomas Simon, one of England's finest medallists, cast and chased an oval copper medal edged with silver and complete with suspension ring in honour of Henry Ireton. On the obverse is Ireton's portrait, with a Latin inscription asking the rhetorical question 'How can he be repaid for all he has done for us!' The reverse is more picturesque: a soldier is climbing a rock and setting fire to some buildings; a battle is raging in the background, and there is an inscription which translates into 'Justice and necessity compel'. Ireton (1610–51) was educated at Oxford; he joined the Roundheads when the war began and fought at the battle of Naseby. In 1646 he married Cromwell's daughter, Bridget. In the year this medal was cast (1650) he was appointed deputy for the Protector in Ireland, and the reverse of the medal refers to his cruel and bloodthirsty methods of subduing the

Irish, the inscription arguing that he was compelled by necessity.

Thomas Simon struck both gold and silver medals to commemorate Cromwell's acceptance of the title of Lord Protector in 1653. On the obverse Cromwell is portrayed wearing armour and a cloak, with a Latin inscription that translates 'Oliver, by the grace of God and the republic of England, Scotland and Ireland, Protector'. The reverse has a lion holding a shield in front of it bearing the Protectorate's arms, with the telling inscription 'Pax quaeritur bello' (Peace is sought by war). Cromwell always considered his victories to be the work of God.

In sharp contrast one Dutch medal issued in 1650 sought to expose Cromwell and Fairfax by portraying their heads, one on each side, in comic cartoon style. But another medal, struck in silver and copper and oval in shape, shows Cromwell in a better light: it is Thomas Simon's Dunbar battle medal of 1650. On the obverse Cromwell is wearing armour, and the battle can just be seen in the distance behind him. The inscription falls into two parts: 'The Lord of Hosts' and 'Word at Dunbar Septem y. 3 1650'. Thomas Simon has engraved his name on Cromwell's arm. The reverse has a picture of Parliament in session with the speaker in his chair. The medal was struck for issue to the officers and soldiers who had taken part in the battle of Dunbar. The battle was fought shortly after Charles II had been proclaimed king in Scotland, and it nearly resulted in a defeat for Cromwell, who found himself hemmed in by the Scots' general, David Leslie. The latter foolishly led his men away from the security of the hill they were on and Cromwell attacked, taking 10,000 prisoners and slaying 3,000. But when he marched north to take Perth, he left the road to England open and Charles II invaded the country.

Charles II faced Cromwell in the crucial battle of Worcester on 3 September 1651. Charles was inside the city and Cromwell approached from the south, making two pontoon bridges from twenty boats which he had collected from Upton-on-Severn to get his men across the 10 yd wide River Teme and the 40 yd wide River Severn. This must have been one of the earliest battles in which emergency bridges were built under fire. After several hours of fighting the king realised the battle was lost and took flight. A lead medal, probably unique, in the British Museum

Page 52, The Early Stuarts (V)
(1) and (2) General Ireton and soldier, 1650; (3) Battle of Worcester, 1651;
(4) Boscobel Oak, 1651; (5) Admiral Blake naval reward, 1653.

records the event. The obverse has a view of the walls and fortifications of Worcester with the defenders seen in their positions.
Outside the walls Charles is to be seen on horseback attended by
the four Penderels and Yates who were to aid him in his escape.
The inscription reads 'Woster. God bles my lord Wilmot, Lady
Lane, Col. Carles, Capt. Tedersal'. These four were also to aid
him in his escape, Carles being a misspelling for Careless, and
Tedersal for Tattersal, the skipper of the ship that eventually
took him over the Channel from Shoreham-by-Sea. The reverse has
a sword and an olive branch crossed between the letters C. and R.
Its Latin inscription, 'In utrumque paratus' implies that Charles
should be prepared for both peace and war.

A second lead medal, also in the British Museum, marks the
time Charles is reputed to have spent hiding in an oak tree at
Boscobel. The obverse shows the famous oak, whose branches
hold three crowns; its inscription reads 'Worth a hapeny. God
did presarve C. R. from Woster. 1651'. The reverse shows a sword
and olive branch crossed between C. R.; above are the words
'Wor brings pece', and below, 'Worth soe much. God bles C. R. in
minding the poore from Frad'.

War with Holland was one of Cromwell's problems but one
he was keen to pursue because of his personal interest in trade and
colonisation, which the Dutch were threatening to undermine.
They had already sold sugar-cane crushers and copper boiling
tanks to the English colonists in the West Indies on hire-purchase
terms, so that the latter could sell them sugar. Cromwell introduced
a policy of mercantilism, the opposite of free trade, to drive them
out. The medals issued to commemorate Admiral Blake's victories
over the Dutch in 1653 do not come within the context of this
book, since they are award medals given to those who participated.
In 1654 peace was made and duly celebrated in medals. One silver
medal struck in Holland shows the figure of Britannia (holding a
harp) and a female figure representing Holland (with a lion at her
feet) jointly holding up a cap of Liberty; the inscription gives the
date of the peace treaty. On the reverse a British ship and a Dutch
ship can be seen sailing peaceably together on a calm sea, with a
Latin inscription which translates 'Commerce, tranquillized by a
double alliance, flourishes on the sea, and the amity of the whole

world welcomes the reconciled'. On the stern of each ship are the letters S.D., for Sebastian Dadler, who designed the medal. He was a native of Strasburg who worked at Augsburg, Nuremberg, Hamburg and Dresden between 1619 and 1653.

A rare silver medal, which was engraved at the time, shows Cromwell standing on a dais and presenting the treaty to the Dutch ambassador; the inscription is in Dutch and reads 'Peace concluded between the Lord Protector Cromwell and the High and Mighty Lords of the States General in the year 1654'. The reverse has the coat of arms of the town of Sluys, and another Dutch inscription, reading 'Peter Lips and Ferdinand de Backere, Burgomasters of the town of Sluys, in the year 1654'. Several other medals commemorate this treaty.

The death of Oliver Cromwell in 1658 was marked by a number of medals, though not all of them are of good quality. One rare oval medal struck in gold and copper shows his bust with short hair, plain collar and armour on the obverse, and a young olive-tree growing close to the dead stump of an old one, with shepherds attending their flocks nearby. Its Latin inscription translates 'They shall not lack an olive-tree. 3 September 1658'. Presumably this implies that Richard Cromwell will serve the people as his father had done. It was struck by Thomas Simon, the eminent engraver.

Chapter Four

The Later Stuarts

THE RESTORATION

From the royalist point of view the reign of Charles II began on the death of his father in 1649, but his effective reign began with his Restoration to the throne in 1660.

The medallists of the period were several, among them Thomas Rawlins, who had followed the royalist cause during the Civil War and who now returned to become the Chief Engraver to the Mint. In spite of his work for Cromwell, Thomas Simon stayed on at the Mint, and he was responsible for the best work done there until his death in 1665. Two Dutch names also appear among the medallists of this time—Pieter van Abeele and John Roettier. The latter was the eldest of three brothers, medallists like their father, a native of Antwerp. John came to England shortly after the Restoration and was employed at the Mint. On 3 July 1669 he and his brothers, Joseph and Philip, were appointed HM Engravers at the Mint with a yearly allowance of £450.

A unique feature of the medallic history of Charles II is that he was the subject of a number of pre-coronation publicity medals issued when it seemed likely that he would be restored to the throne. One of Thomas Simon's lead medals has the sun rising from the sea on the reverse as a symbol of his expected and hoped-for return, and its obverse bears his portrait in armour. A similar symbolic scene appears on another of his medals, a silver one struck in 1660. Above three crowns hanging on the branches of a leafless oak tree the sun is dispersing the clouds. Its Latin inscription translates 'At last it grows strong again'. The three crowns are probably the crowns of England, Scotland and Ireland, though they could be taken as those of the three Stuart kings. A similar cast and chased silver oval medal was issued with the inscription 'Carolus Secundus' on the other side; as it has a ring for suspension it was probably designed to be worn to celebrate the return of the king.

Besides these medals, two were issued in Holland by Pieter van Abeele. The first has the bust of Charles I dressed in doublet and lace collar on the obverse, and Charles II in a doublet and wearing a medal on the reverse; this silver medal consists of two plates united by the rim. The other depicts Charles II in armour with the badge of the Garter on the obverse, and William III of Holland on horseback, against the background of a river and city, on the reverse. This, too, is a silver medal made in the same way as Abeele's first.

A unique gold medal in the British Museum, cast and chased in Holland, with a suspension ring, shows the bust of Charles II in armour on the obverse, while on the reverse are three crowns within branches of laurel and palm, with the inscription 'Propter strenvitatem et fidelitatem rebus in adversis' ('For steadfastness and faithfulness in adverse circumstances'). Presumably it was given to some particularly faithful follower of Charles II.

Pieter van Abeele was responsible for the repoussé and chased silver medal issued to commemorate Charles's embarkation at Scheveningen on 23 May 1660. The obverse has the portrait of the king in armour, while the reverse shows the fleet in full sail, above which the figure of Fame is seen with a trumpet and scroll. Underneath this picture is a Dutch inscription giving the date of departure as 2 June, which it was according to the New Style calendar used by the Dutch. The ship which Charles sailed in was the *Naseby*, but its name was altered to the *Royal Charles* in honour of its passenger.

John Roettier struck the silver medal commemorating Charles's landing at Dover. The obverse depicts the king wearing armour, set within laurel and surrounded by the inscription '1660 Die 29 Maii', which is in fact the date of his entry into London, as he had landed on 25 May. The reverse has a ship approaching the shore on which England, Scotland and Ireland are personified

Page 57, The Later Stuarts (I)
(1) Charles II embarks, 1660; (2) Charles II lands, 1660; (3) Charles II's
Coronation, 1661; (4) and (5) The Plague and Fire of London, 1666.

with three crowns, a sceptre and a sword waiting to greet the king. Above the ship is the star and eye of Providence, and in the distance Dover Castle. The Latin inscription translates 'If God is the protector, who will be my enemy'. Charles landed at about 1pm, and while the barge was carrying the king's party ashore, one of the king's dogs fouled the boat—which, wrote Samuel Pepys, 'made us laugh, and methink that a King and all that belong to him are but just as others are'. General Monck received the king, and was duly knighted for his services in bringing about the restoration. John Evelyn described Charles's entrance into London:

> 29. This day came in His Majestie Charles the 2d to London after a sad, & Long Exile and Calamitous Suffering both of the King & Church: being 17 years: This was also his Birthday, and with a Triumph of above 20000 horse & foote, brandishing their swords and shouting with unexpressable joy: The wayes straw'd with flowers, the bells ringing, the streetes hung with Tapissry, fountaines running with wine . . . [the procession] was 7 hours in passing the Citty, even from 2 in the afternone 'til nine at night.

The Restoration was marked by bonfires which caused a national coal shortage and the issue of several medals, among them a silver one struck by the only Englishman, George Bower, capable of competing with the Roettiers. It is known as the 'Gigantomachia' medal, and shows the king in Garter robes on the obverse with the inscription 'Carolus II dei gratis mag. Br.&c', and Jupiter, carried through the clouds on an eagle, striking giants with thunderbolts. This scene probably refers to the execution of the regicides, the men directly responsible for Charles I's death. Another well known Restoration silver medal is the 'Felicitas Britanniae' ('Fortune of Britain'), struck by John Roettier. The obverse has the portrait of the king dressed in armour and a cloak, while the reverse has the figure of Peace with scales and fasces, accompanied by Minerva and Hercules, presenting an olive-branch to Britannia, who is seated on the seashore. Behind the group is Fame, and, above it, Genius. The inscription reads 'Felicitas Britanniae 29 Maii 1660'. Minerva represents the arts and Hercules strength, and the scene is intended to suggest that the Restoration is providential, bringing with it justice, peace and plenty. A similar Roettier medal struck in gold has the figures of Hercules, Minerva, Peace and Mercury (with the features of Charles) assembled round an altar, behind which stands Prudence leaning on a shield with Britannia, while Plenty reposes in the foreground.

Roettier was responsible for a slightly belated Restoration medal known as 'Favente Deo', struck in gold in 1667. On the obverse is the king, while the reverse has Britannia, holding spear and shield, seated on the seashore watching the navy. It is inscribed 'Favente Deo' ('By God's favour'), while round the edge are the words 'Carolus secundus pacis et imperii restitutor augustus'. (Charles II, august restorer of peace and authority'.) Samuel Pepys wrote in his diary for 26 February 1667:

> At my goldsmith's did observe the King's new medall where in little there is Mrs Stewart's face as well done as ever I saw any thing in my whole life, I think: and a pretty thing it is that he should choose her face to represent Brittannia by.

Mrs Stuart, later Duchess of Richmond, was one of the court beauties of the day, and the king's mistress.

Two medals were issued to commemorate the coronation, which took place on 23 April 1661. Curiously enough, they were both by Thomas Simon and not by Roettier or George Bower. The first was struck in gold and silver for distribution among those present. The obverse depicts the king wearing his crown and dressed in the robes of the Garter, while the reverse has the king seated on a chair, or throne, wearing the crown and holding the sceptre while the winged figure of Peace (or Victory) hovers overhead touching the crown. The inscription on the reverse translates 'Sent to support a fallen age 23 April 1661'. The second medal was cast and chased in both gold and silver, the king appearing in Garter robes with a laurel on his head; the reverse had an oak tree in full leaf with three crowns on its branches, and the sun shining down. The Latin inscription translates 'Already it flourishes, 23 April 1661'. The fact that the oak tree is in full leaf, implying a successful restoration, contrasts with the leafless oak-tree design of the medal anticipating Charles's return. This later medal has a loop for suspension and appears to have been hastily produced for distribution to Charles's servants, for there is a record in Simon's accounts saying that he supplied two gold versions for the king's cooks.

A year later Charles married Catherine of Braganza, daughter of John IV of Portugal, which led to the issuing of half a dozen different medals, George Bower being responsible for four of them. One, in silver-gilt, has the busts of the king and queen facing each other and, on the reverse, the figure of Fame holding a trumpet and an olive-branch. The second, in silver, has the busts of the king and queen on the obverse, and on the reverse shows Jupiter and Venus (with Cupid behind them), with the inscription 'Majestas et amor' ('majesty and love'). Bower's third, also oval and struck in silver, has the crowned figure of the king in armour on the obverse, and the queen wearing a coronet on the reverse. His last marriage medal was of similar design but round. One oval medal cast and chased in silver with a suspension loop, and made by an unknown person, has the portrait of Catherine with her hair drawn back and wearing a coronet, in a Portugese-style dress. Soon after she came to England she adopted the English style of dress, which means that this medal must have been issued when she first arrived. On its reverse are two orange trees with their stems intertwined. The finest marriage medal, however, was that struck by J. Roettier and known as the 'Golden Medal'; it was also struck in silver, copper and copper-gilt. On the obverse is Charles laureated, wearing armour and a cloak, and on the reverse is the queen, her hair ornamented with pearls. It was of this medal that the poet Waller wrote:

> Our guard upon the royal side
> On the reverse, our beauty's pride!
> Here we discern the frown and smile
> The force and glory of our isle.

WARS AND TREATIES

Among medals of this period concerning international events is one by J. Mauger recording the sale of Dunkirk to Louis XIV in 1662. In silver, its obverse has the portrait of Louis, described in Latin as a most Christian king, while the reverse shows Dunkirk, represented by a female figure, kneeling and presenting the keys of the city to Louis against a background of a galley with a shield bearing the arms of Dunkirk. It had been captured by Cromwell, but Charles found the upkeep of its complicated defences too expensive and was glad to sell it for £200,000. In England blame for the sale was put on the Earl of Clarendon, the king's chief minister, and he was accused of using some of the money to help pay for the £50,000 house he built near the present Piccadilly Circus. The house was christened 'Dunkirk House' by his opponents.

The Second Dutch War, 1665–7, in which the Dutch fought off Charles's attempt to enforce his mercantile policy of preventing them from trading with Britain's colonies, can be said to have been Britain's first truly colonial war; and it witnessed the issuing of a number of patriotic medals by both contestants. The battle off Lowestoft on 3 June 1665 in which James, Duke of York, commanded a fleet which sank sixteen Dutch ships and captured nine more, with the loss of 2,000 lives, was the subject of the English medals. The English ships were heavier and better suited to the ocean weather than the flatter-bottomed Dutch ships. Officers of the rank of captain and above were given commemorative gold or silver medals struck by Roettier; the king wearing a mantle appeared on the obverse, and in Roman military uniform viewing the naval action from the shore on the reverse. The inscription on the reverse translates 'For signal daring'. John Roettier also struck a silver medal celebrating the Duke of York himself: it depicts him wearing armour and a cloak on the obverse with an inscription stressing his status as High Admiral of England, and the reverse depicts the battle in progress with the Duke's flagship in the foreground. Besides the date of the battle the inscription translates 'Not less on land', implying that the duke was as great a soldier as he was a sailor. This medal is probably Roettier's finest work.

In the same year, 1665, Thomas Simon struck his last medal—the 'Dominion of the Sea' medal in silver. It is small and shows his skill at producing minute detail. On the obverse is the bust of Charles II, and the reverse depicts the king as Neptune holding a trident and riding in a chariot drawn by four seahorses, against the background of the fleet. The inscription on the reverse translates 'The sea shall be his slave'. Three Dutch medals struck in 1665 and 1666 gave considerable offence to Charles; he referred to them when he wished to renew the war in 1672, and described them as 'false historical medals'. This bluntness was not, in fact, justified, though it is true to say that the medals were strongly propagandist. The first two were issued by Jerian Pool by orders of the Dutch government. On 10 August 1665 a naval action was fought in

Bergen harbour when the Earl of Sandwich sailed in with fifteen men of war, four small vessels and two fireships. Pool's silver medal to commemorate what followed shows Bergen on the obverse with the fight going on in the harbour, and his own name inscribed below; the reverse is covered in an inscription in Dutch to the effect that Sandwich's fleet had chased ten Dutch East Indiamen into the harbour, formed his fleet into a crescent to surround them, then fled as the harbour forts and the Dutch ships opened fire.

The second of Pool's silver medals has also been attributed to another Dutch medallist, Christoffel Adolfszoon, and was struck to commemorate the Four Days' Battle that took place off the North Foreland on 1–4 June 1666. It was one of the bloodiest battles ever fought, involving 150 ships; the English lost 23 ships, 5,000 dead and 2–3,000 prisoners, and the Dutch 6–7 ships and 2,000 men. The outcome was indecisive, as dense fog ended the fight. On the obverse the naval engagement is depicted and on the reverse a Latin inscription states that the medal was issued officially by the States-General as a memorial to the splendid victory achieved by Dutch valour, leading to the capture of an admiral (Sir George Ayscue) and the sinking of twenty-three ships.

The third silver medal that annoyed the king was Adolfszoon's 'Peace of Breda', struck in 1667 to mark the ending of the war. On the obverse is the figure of Holland, 'gentle and brave', trampling on Discord, with a lion and lamb at her feet, while in the distance there is a view of Breda and ships in flames. The Latin inscription reads: 'Procul hinc mala bestia regnis Jun 22 1667', this reference to a wicked beast ('mala bestia') ruling from afar ('procul') being taken by Charles to refer to himself. The reverse depicts the figure of Peace holding a sword and wreath and trampling on arms and a crown, while from the clouds above an outstretched hand holds the shields of England and Holland, and merchant ships can be seen in the distance. The Latin inscription, to the effect that peace has now been divinely established after a period of angry war, is dated 31 August 1667. Round the edge there is another inscription stating that the medal was struck by permission of the States-General. Charles's protests were not ignored; he received an apology and the dies of this medal were destroyed.

Earlier, while progress at the peace conference at Breda was slow, the Dutch decided to force the pace of the negotiations by a daring attack up the Medway to the docks at Chatham, an action made the subject of a silver medal by Pieter van Abeele. On the night of 10 June 1667 the Dutch stormed Sheerness and the next day twenty of their ships sailed up the Medway past the guardships, which lacked any ammunition to resist them, broke the chain boom across Chatham harbour, set fire to five warships and towed away the *Royal Charles*, the 80 gun ship that had brought Charles to England in 1660. London in particular was thunder-struck. A Quaker ran through Westminster Hall, London, naked except for a cloth 'civilly tied about the privities to avoid scandall', with a dish of burning coals on his head, crying 'Repent', while John Evelyn wrote in his *Diary*:

> This alarm caused me to send away my best goods, plate, etc, from my house to another place. The alarm was so great that it put both county and city in panic, fear, and consternation such as I hope I shall never see more. Everybody was flying, none knew why or whither.

Abeele's medal shows the burning of the English ships in the Medway, the Dutch inscription stating that their ships were ordered to attack the English ships near Chatham, and to burn and sink them. On the reverse is the figure of Peace with an olive branch and cornucopiae seated between the shields of England, France and Denmark on the one side and those of the United Provinces on the other, while below is the date, 6 September 1667, when the peace treaty was proclaimed. It had been signed on 31 July.

The treaty of Breda was the subject of a number of other medals issued by Dutch engravers, some of which show views of Breda and others of ships or Neptune.

The Third Dutch War, 1672–4, has few medals to commemorate it. A French silver medal struck by J. Mauger in honour of the battle of Solebay, 28 May 1672, carries the head of Louis XIV on the obverse and Neptune in a sea-chariot threatening the personified figure of Holland with his trident on the reverse. The battle was fought in foggy conditions between 150 allied ships and 88 Dutch. The Duke of York and Lord Sandwich found themselves surrounded on the *Royal James*, which lost 300 men before a great fireship, disguised as a battleship with dummy guns and men, set fire to her, so blowing her up. The Duke survived, half blinded by the

1

3

4

Page 64, The Later Stuarts (II)
(1) Naval engagement, 1–4 June, 1666; (2) Medway ships burning, 1667;
(3) Duchess of Portsmouth, 1673; (4) British Colonisation, 1670; (5) Rye
House Plot, 1683.

smoke and his wig singed, but Lord Sandwich's body was found ten days later in the water, eaten by porpoises, identifiable only from the Garter star it was wearing. The peace treaty signed in London in 1674 was commemorated by a Dutch silver medal depicting William of Orange on horseback with his troops bombarding a town by the sea in the background; on the reverse a dove is flying over a calm sea and ships can be seen in the distance.

DOMESTIC EVENTS

Turning to more domestic events, the plague and fire of London are commemorated by only one medal, in silver, struck in 1666. The subject of the obverse is the reward of goodness, which is symbolised by peace and plenty: a shrine with a crucifix stands between a vineyard and a cornfield above which the sun, named Jehovah, shines, and beneath which St Paul removes the plague (symbolised by a viper), while a tree springs to life again beside him. The reverse has a view across the Thames of London half in flames and half under a rain storm, while the eye of Providence looks down between comets and a gale of wind; in the foreground Death and a soldier on horseback are engaged in combat.

In 1673 J. Roettier struck a silver medal to commemorate Charles II's endowment of a mathematical and nautical school at Christ's Hospital. John Evelyn referred to it as a 'glorious medallion'. Its obverse has a portrait of the king in decorated armour and a cloak, and a Bluecoat Schoolboy surrounded by Arithmetic, Astronomy, Mathematics and Mercury, each with their instruments, while in the distance some ships can be seen. Another medal in honour of the foundation bears a problem in geometry. Christ's Hospital had been founded in the previous century for orphans in good physical condition who were the sons of London freemen. Charles gave £7,000 towards the building and settled an income of £370 per annum on it to provide for forty boys, ten of whom were to be annually sent out to start a seafaring career. In 1731 Don Manoel Gonzales wrote in his London guidebook:

> The children are dieted in the following manner: They have every morning for their breakfast bread and beer, at half an hour past six in the morning in the summer time, and at half an hour past seven in

the winter. On Sundays they have boiled beef and broth for their dinners, and for their suppers legs and shoulders of mutton. On Tuesdays and Thursdays they have the same dinners as on Sundays, that is, boiled beef and broth; on the other days no flesh meat, but on Mondays milkporridge, on Wednesdays furmity, on Fridays old pease and pottage, on Saturdays water-gruel. They have roast beef about twelve days in the year by the kindness of several benefactors, who have left, some £3, some 50s per annum, for that end. Their supper is bread and cheese, or butter for those who cannot eat cheese; only Wednesdays and Fridays they have pudding-pies for supper.

The diet of these children seems to be exceeding mean and sparing; and I have heard some of their friends say that it would not be easy for them to subsist upon it without their assistance. However, it is observed they are very healthful; that out of eleven or twelve hundred there are scarce ever found twelve in the sick ward; and that in one year, when there were upwards of eleven hundred in this hospital, there were not more than fifteen of them died. Besides, their living in this thrifty parsimonious manner, makes them better capable of shifting for themselves when they come out into the world.

The boys at Christ's Hospital today still wear their famous bluecoat uniform with orange stockings, but their diet has much improved.

The so-called Popish Plot of 1678 was the subject of half a dozen medals concentrating on the murder of the magistrate Sir Edmund Berry Godfrey. In that year Titus Oates, who claimed to be a doctor of divinity from Salamanca University but who had in fact been expelled from his school, his naval chaplaincy and from a Jesuit college but not from Cambridge, joined forces with Dr Israel Tonge, a famous Oxford botanist, to present evidence that there was a popish plot to put Charles's brother, James, Duke of York, on the throne. Charles was to be murdered either by poison administered to him by the queen's doctor, or by a Jesuit priest stabbing him in the park. Oates and Tonge had reported the plot to Sir Edmund Berry Godfrey, who was then murdered, by Catholics it was suggested, in order to prevent him from disclosing the information he had received. He was strangled at the watergate at Somerset House, then his body was taken to Primrose Hill and left in a ditch transfixed with his own sword. Charles interrogated Oates himself and soon caught him out on his descriptions of some of the conspirators, but realising the popular anger against the Catholics called for some action against them, he allowed the trials and executions of some Catholics to take place. His Chancellor,

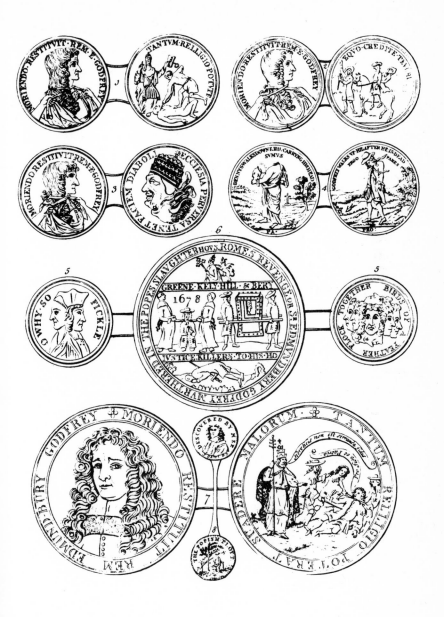

Page 67, The Later Stuarts (III)
The murder of Sir Edmund Berry Godfrey, 1678
(1) Jesuit murders Godfrey; (2) The body disposed of; (3) Pope-Devil;
(4) The legend of St Denis' martyrdom; (5) 'O why so fickle?'; (6) Rome's
revenge; (7) The murder; (8) The ambush: Titus Oates discovers the plot.

Lord Shaftesbury, tried to incriminate the Catholics by attempting to bribe a coachman into saying that the conspirators had used his coach to convey Godfrey's body to Primrose Hill, combining an offer of £500 with a threat to put him in a barrel of nails and roll him down a hill if he declined. The man refused the bribe and was chained up in Newgate prison for his honesty. The outcome was that the Duke of York, heir to the throne, had to go into exile and the Second Test Act was passed, preventing Catholics from becoming Members of Parliament.

A cast and chased pewter medal, plain on the reverse, depicts the murder of Godfrey. It is divided into three parts. The centre shows two monks strangling Godfrey, above whom is the date 1678, and two men are shown carrying the body in a sedan chair; above are the names 'Greene, Kely, Hill & Bery', while below is the inscription 'Justice killers to his ho[liness]'. In the lower part Godfrey is to be seen lying on his face, his sword passed through his body. In the upper part the Pope is being prompted by the devil with the inscription 'Romes revenge or Sr Edmundbery Godfrey murthered in the popes slaughter hous'. Another medal, struck in silver by G. Bower, shows the bust of Godfrey being strangled by two hands with his own cravat on the obverse, and on the reverse Green strangling Godfrey in the presence of the Pope, who is holding a papal bull and blessing the murder. A Latin inscription round the edge compares Godfrey to Atlas: the latter required all his strength to sustain the world, while Godfrey's strength lay in his faith. Bower also struck a silver medal with the same obverse; its reverse, however, showed Hill on horseback supporting the dead body of Godfrey, accompanied by another conspirator feigning drunkenness and carrying a sword, on their way to Primrose Hill (in the background) at night under the stars. Apparently the murderers had agreed to pretend that they were a party of drunkards if seen by anyone as they conveyed Godfrey's body to the hill. Greene, Hill and Berry were hung in 1679 on perjured evidence.

A third medal by Bower, also struck in silver, depicts Godfrey walking after his murder, with the inscription 'Godfrey walks up hil after hee is dead'. On the reverse St Denis is shown after his martyrdom carrying his own head, with the words 'Dennys walks downe hil carrying his head'. This medal was struck after it was reported that Godfrey's ghost had been seen on Primrose Hill, and the implication is that Godfrey was a Protestant saint, to the extent that St Denis was a Catholic saint. On this fourth Popish Plot medal Bower produced a Janus-head—a Jesuit's face with a cap backed by a monk's with a cowl—inscribed 'O why so fickle'; while on the reverse is a cluster of seven heads and the words 'Birds of a feather flock together'. It is not clear who is meant to be represented; Evelyn thought the double head represented Titus Oates and Bedloe, a Chepstow horse-thief who claimed he knew all about the murder, and that the cluster of heads comprised those of the men who had detected the plot. But it is possible that the seven heads are those of Charles, James and the king's five leading ministers.

Finally, one silver-gilt medal depicts Godfrey being strangled by two hands on the obverse, and the Pope's head and the devil's joined into one face on the reverse, with an inscription which translates 'The church perverted shows the devil's face'.

In the years following the Popish Plot Lord Shaftesbury attacked the Roman Catholic Duke of York in order to prevent him succeeding to the throne when Charles II died, but in 1681 Charles struck back by denouncing the anti-James movement and arresting Shaftesbury for high treason. To Charles's chagrin Shaftesbury was acquitted, and this was the occasion for G. Bower striking a silver medal for Shaftesbury's supporters. The obverse bears a portrait of Shaftesbury wearing a cloak, while the reverse shows the sun appearing from behind a cloud over London, with the Latin inscription 'Laetamur' ('Let us rejoice') and the date of the acquittal. Just over 100 years later several radicals acquitted on treason charges adopted the same way of publicising their release. Shaftesbury's medal is described by Dryden in his poem *The Medal*.

According to Spence's *Anecdotes* Charles II is said to have given Dryden the idea of writing a poem about the medal. Spence wrote: 'One day, as the king was walking in the Mall, and talking with Dryden, he said, "If I was a poet, and I think I am poor enough to be one, I would write a poem on such a subject, in the following manner".' He then gave Dryden a plan for the poem.

When Dryden published it in March 1682, he gave it the subtitle of
'A Satire against Sedition'. One verse read:

> Power was his aim; but, thrown from that pretence,
> The wretch turned loyal in his own defence,
> And malice reconciled him to his prince,
> Him in the anguish of his soul he served,
> Rewarded faster still than he deserved.
> Behold him, now exalted into trust;
> His counsels oft convenient, seldom just;
> Even in the most sincere advice he gave
> He had a grudging still to be a knave.
> The frauds he learnt in his fanatic years
> Made him uneasy in his lawful gears.
> At best as little honest as he could:
> And, like white witches, mischievously good.
> To his first bias, longingly he leans;
> And rather would be great by wicked means.
> . . . . . .
> When he just sovereign by no impious way
> Could be seduced to arbitrary sway,
> Forsaken of that hope, he shifts his sail;
> Drives down the current with a popular gale;
> And shows the fiend confessed without a veil.
> He preaches to the crowd that power is lent,
> But not conveyed to kingly government.

A rather poor silver medal struck by Bower in 1683 to commemorate the discovery of the Rye House Plot has Charles, nude in the
form of Hercules, reclining on a lion's skin and feebly warding off a
Hydra with seven human heads; Windsor Castle lies in the distance
and thunder is striking over it. The reverse has a shepherd seated
on a mound watching his flock, and two wolves are to be seen
hanging on a nearby gibbet; London is visible in the distance, and
a dove with an olive branch flies overhead. On the obverse the
Latin inscription reads 'They are destroyed by a stroke of lightning',
and on the reverse 'God gave us this peace'. The heads on the
Hydra are those of the devil, the Duke of Monmouth, Lord Russell,
John Hampden, Algernon Sidney, the Earl of Essex and Lord
Howard, Whig leaders indirectly involved in the plot. The two
wolves are Algernon Sidney and Lord Russell, who were executed.
The plot was to ambush the king and the Duke of York as they

left the Newmarket races and passed by Rye House, and then to crown Charles's illegitimate son, the Duke of Monmouth. A careless groom set fire to the racecourse buildings halfway through the week's races, so the royal brothers rode home several days earlier than expected, with the result that the plot misfired. In fact the king knew nothing of it until some time afterwards, when a bankrupt oil-merchant confessed to what he knew. Some of the conspirators were executed though the evidence against them was flimsy.

Two years later, in 1683, Bower struck a silver medal to com-memorate the marriage of the Duke of York's daughter Anne (later Queen Anne), to Prince George of Denmark. The obverse has the portraits of George in armour and Anne, draped, facing each other, while the reverse has an oak tree with acorns on the ground round it, and a Latin inscription implying that the house of Stuart will give protection to their descendants.

In 1685 two interesting medals were struck to mark the research work of Sir Samuel Morland into the possibilities of a steam engine. A brass medal depicts a conical-shaped engine on a square wooden base floating on the sea. Steam comes from a long pipe emerging from the side of the engine, while in the distance a ship in full sail can be seen. The Latin inscription translates 'The sea and fire accord'. On the reverse is a boat carrying a conical-shaped engine, similar to that on the obverse but this time standing on a tripod; rain is falling in the distance. The inscription translates 'Art emulating heaven'. The other medal is made of pewter with a similar obverse, apart from the inscription; the reverse, however, has an ornamental fountain, and two ships, with a Latin inscription— 'The water will be the more welcome the less it is expected'. Sir Samuel Morland, Master of Mechanics, was fascinated by the possibilities of steam power and of pumps. He succeeded in bringing water from Blackmoor Park, near Winkfield, to the top of Windsor Castle. The engine shown on the medal was his fire-engine, patented in 1675 and based on Cyprian Lucar's of 1590. The medals were properly struck by Isaac Thompson, the King's Engine-maker and Morland's employee, who advertised the fact that he could make all kinds of pumps for private houses and ships, fire-engines, engines for wetting ship's sails, small engines for watering gardens and brass engines for 'playing water in fountains'.

Charles's death in 1685 was the subject of a few medals, of which only one, probably by the Dutchman Van Loon, need concern us. It was struck in silver and carries a rather poor portrait of the king wearing a lion's skin on the obverse, and the setting sun on the reverse, with the inscription 'Omnia orta occidunt' ('Nothing born but must die').

We cannot leave the medallic history of Charles's long reign without mentioning two medals struck in honour of his mistresses. Bower produced a silver one in honour of Lucie, Duchess of Portsmouth, whose bust is shown on the obverse; the reverse shows Cupid seated upon the globe, with the inscription 'Omnia vincit', implying that love conquers all. Lucie de Querouaille was made Duchess of Portsmouth in 1673. The other medal was the work of J. Roettier, in copper with a plain reverse. Its obverse shows the bust of Frances Stuart, Duchess of Richmond, wearing classical dress. Daughter of Walter Stuart and wife of the fourth Duke of Richmond, she was one of the greatest beauties at Charles's court, and outlived him, to die in 1702.

A few medals were struck in the reigns of Charles and James for presentation to people whom they had 'touched' for the king's evil; it was claimed that the King's touch could cure a form of scrofula. They would be hung round the touched person's neck on a white ribbon. A gold medal struck in 1661 has a ship in full sail on the obverse, and St Michael and the dragon on the reverse. James had similar medals struck in silver as well as gold, and his son, the Old Pretender, did so as well in 1710. The ceremony of 'touching' was dropped by George I, who, on receiving a supplicant's request to perform the ceremony on his son, replied that he would do better to approach the Old Pretender!

JAMES II AND MARY

Opinions differ as to the quality of the medals struck by J. Roettier to commemorate the accession and coronation of James II and Queen Mary in 1685. He invariably struck his medals rather than cast them, which, according to some, sharpened their outlines and brought out their fine portraiture. Others have argued that these medals are in very low relief, with little modelling, and the result is that only dull outline portraits adorn them. His gold and silver medals honouring the queen, which on the obverse show her wearing laurels, and draped, and on the reverse personifying Venus seated on a mound, hardly justify the motto 'O dea certe' ('Certainly a goddess'). The king's gold medal (also issued in silver and copper) depicts him duly wearing laurels, cloaked, and, on the reverse, a laurel-wreath on a cushion and a hand holding a crown protruding from a cloud. The inscription translates 'From the camp to the throne', alluding to James's past military career. The reverse of the queen's medal and the obverse of the king's were also struck as one medal, both in gold and silver, to commemorate their accession. The king's medal is scarce today, but the silver version of the queen's is not uncommon.

G. Bower also produced a coronation medal in silver-gilt and silver, more impressive than Roettier's coronation medals though cold and hard like all Bower's work. On the obverse are the busts of the king and queen, while the reverse has the face of the sun radiating its rays in all directions, with the Latin inscription 'Shining in strength yet kindly'.

The Scottish parliament met on the day of the king's coronation, 23 April 1685, and this assembly was marked by the striking of a silver medal by Jan Smeltzing, which depicts the head of the king on the obverse, and a lion couchant, crowned and holding a sceptre and orb, on the reverse. Its Latin inscription translates 'Touch me at your peril'. Smeltzing, who was born at Nimeguen, worked most of his life at Leyden, but was forced to leave there because of his satirical medals, mention of which will be made later.

James's troubled reign was only to last three years, and for the superstitious this was foreshadowed by three incidents during his coronation day—the crown nearly fell off his head during the ceremony, the canopy held over him collapsed, and the royal standard blew off the mast of the White Tower. Within a few months the Duke of Monmouth, Charles II's illegitimate son, landed with eighty men at Lyme Regis in Dorset to raise an army of some 5,000 countryfolk and march towards the capital, but he was overwhelmed at Sedgemoor in July. He escaped, only to be captured, brought to London and executed—an unwise move, for it gave James's opponents a chance to choose a new leader,

Page 74, The Later Stuarts (IV)
(1) and (2) Monmouth's Rebellion, 1685; (3) The Trial of the Seven Bishops, 1688; (4) and (5) The Trial of the Seven Bishops—the Catholic undermining of the church.

William of Orange. Naturally this rebellion was the subject of a number of medals, some pro-James and others pro-Monmouth.

The medals supporting James were struck by Bower, Roettier and Arondeaux. Bower produced a silver medal with the bust of Monmouth wearing armour on the obverse and a more elaborate reverse: Monmouth falling from a rock into the sea in an attempt to reach the three crowns of England, Scotland and Ireland, which are on a rock together with a palm and laurel branches. Bower struck another with the same obverse, and on the reverse two genii in the clouds supporting a coronet above the cipher 'J.E.D.M.' (James Edward, Duke of Monmouth) and the inscription 'Caput inter nubila' ('Head in the clouds'). Roettier's was a silver medal, more in the form of a naval or military award for loyalists. Its obverse has the bust of James and its reverse some fighting equipment and a naval battle in the background. R. Arondeaux, a French medallist who later worked for William III, struck a silver medal to commemorate the beheading of Monmouth and Argyll. The obverse depicts James's bust on a pedestal resting on the four sceptres of England, Scotland, Ireland and France, with ships and Neptune in a sea-chariot in the background. The reverse has Justice holding a sword and weighing three crowns against a sword, torch and serpent, while at her feet are the bodies of Monmouth and Argyll, their heads on blocks inscribed with their names; in the distance lightning can be seen destroying troops, and the Tower of London is also shown decorated with heads on spears. The Latin inscription on the reverse points the moral that those who aspire to wickedness will be ruined. Argyll had been responsible for rebellion in Scotland while Monmouth was leading his campaign in the south-west.

Jan Smeltzing struck two silver medals championing Monmouth's lost cause. The first shows the head of Monmouth with the inscription, 'Jacobus infelix dux Monumethensis' ('James, the unfortunate Duke of Monmouth'). The reverse has the decapitated head of Monmouth on the ground spouting blood, with the inscription 'Hunc sanguinem libo deo liberatori' ('The libation offered to God the Deliverer'), followed by the date of the Duke's execution. The second medal has the head of Monmouth on the obverse with an inscription proclaiming him the defender of the faith and freedom of England, while the reverse has a Roman soldier attempting to tear open a lion's jaw, the Latin inscription being to the effect that he tried hard but achieved little.

Smeltzing uncovered the heart of James's problem when he lampooned the king's Catholicism on a silver medal struck in 1688. The obverse shows the altar of Britannia heaped with Catholic emblems such as a dove, chalice, wafer, rosary and mitre, with a Bible in the centre surmounted by a cap inscribed 'libert'; over this scene a hand from a cloud holds out a scroll with the wording, 'C. Fagelii epistola efflagitata a J. Stewardo, 1687' ('The letter of C. Fagel extorted by J. Steward'). This inscription refers to James's employment of James Steward, a Scottish lawyer, to write letters to Fagel to persuade William and Mary of Holland to approve the abolition of the Test Acts and other penal laws against Catholics and Nonconformists. The point Smeltzing is making on the obverse of his medal is that Britain allows religious toleration, since the mitre represents the church of England; the chalice, wafer and rosary the church of Rome; and the dove the Nonconformists with the free Bible at their centre. But on the reverse a dog is shown wearing a rosary and swallowing a book inscribed 'M.I.' (for 'magnum juramentum'), trampling on another marked 'L.C.' (for 'libertas conscientiae'), and throwing down a third marked 'S.R.P.' (for 'salue religionis protestantis') from an ornamented column. James is represented by the dog, devouring his coronation oath, trampling on the liberty of conscience and removing the Test Acts and penal laws, which guarantee the safety of the state.

When James decided to enlist the Nonconformists in his effort to break the hold of the Church of England, by issuing a second Declaration of Indulgence suspending the penal laws affecting Roman Catholics and Nonconformists, and ordered that it should be read in all churches, he was faced with a clerical revolt led by the Archbishop of Canterbury and the bishops of St Asaph, Bath & Wells, Ely, Chichester, Peterborough and Bristol. The fact that these moderate church leaders had abandoned the accepted doctrine of passive obedience and non-resistance to a divinely appointed king marked a clear break in the alliance of church and state. James ordered their trial on a charge of seditious libel, and the resulting 'Trial of the Seven Bishops' in 1688 was recorded by a number of medals. The real issue at stake was whether a king had power to dispense with parliamentary laws, and the bishops' conviction or acquittal would largely settle that vital point. London was jubilant when their acquittal was announced.

Bower struck two medals commemorating the trial, both having the same obverse—a bust of Archbishop Sancroft wearing his robes. This portrait has more life and character than most of Bower's medallic portraits, though it is poor in detail. The reverse of the first medal has a circle of medallions depicting the heads of six bishops and that of the bishop of London in the centre. The six in the circle are those who were tried with the Archbishop, while the presence of the bishop of London in the centre refers to Bishop Compton, who had been suspended from the Privy Council and the deanery of the Chapel Royal in 1685 for his opposition to the king. The other medal's reverse has the group of seven stars known as the Pleiades. A Dutch cast and chased silver medal of coarse workmanship has the picture of a Jesuit and a monk trying to undermine the Church of England, which is founded on a rock and supported by a hand from heaven; its inscription reads 'The gates of hell shall not prevaile'. The reverse has medallions of the seven bishops, and is inscribed 'Wisdom hath builded her hous she hath hewen out her 7 pillers', (a quotation from *Proverbs*, ix, 1).

Jan Smeltzing struck an interesting silver medal showing the White Tower of the Tower of London, with a distant view of the bishops approaching under guard, and the names of the seven together with the dates of their imprisonment and of their release. The reverse has the sun and moon equally balanced on scales suspended from the clouds, probably implying that the king and the people are equally balanced. Finally there was one more silver medal struck by Bower, the bust of Archbishop Sancroft on the obverse, and the church on a rock in the sea, buffeted by four winds, with the words 'Immota triumphans' ('Triumphantly unmoved'), on the reverse, words also used on one of Charles I's memorial medals.

Even before the trial of the bishops was over the nation was faced with another major incident in the power struggle, the birth of the king's son, James (III), later known as the Old Pretender. If he was the genuine son of the king and queen, the Whig protestant

Page 78, The Later Stuarts (V)

The Birth of the Old Pretender, 1688.

(1) The cradle; (2) The babe; (3) 'The Trojan Horse'—a Jesuit plot;
(4) The birth; (5) Ambassador Wood's commemoration of the birth;
(6) The flight of Prince James; (7) The Religious State of England; (8) The
Anti-Christian Confederacy of the Sultan of Turkey, Louis XIV, the Bey
of Algiers and James II.

cause would have no course of action left but rebellion, and an invitation to William of Orange and Mary to assume the throne. Efforts to discredit the genuineness of the royal birth took the forms of medal-issuing, pamphlet-writing and ballad-production. The famous story of the baby being smuggled from a nearby convent in a warming pan has been exhaustively investigated by historians. The use of a warming pan in June, the fact that the wealthy midwife appeared plainly dressed when giving evidence of the birth, and the queen's use of a large enclosed bed instead of a low one, have all been examined. William Fuller claimed in a pamphlet that the child's parents were Mrs Mary Grey and Lord Tyrconnel, and for this suggestion he was punished by three appearances in the pillory, thirty-nine lashes, six months' hard labour and a fine of 1,000 marks. James tactlessly persued his Catholic course by choosing the Pope as his son's godfather.

A Dutch silver medal by Smeltzing shows the nude figure of Truth opening the door of a cabinet to reveal a Jesuit thrusting a baby with a pyx and crown through a trapdoor, which is inscribed with the baby's name and a Latin inscription to the effect that this is the way to secure the succession. The reverse has a Trojan horse with a saddlecloth bearing a Latin inscription which translates 'Liberty of conscience without the oath and penal laws'. This probably refers to James allowing Catholics and Nonconformists to hold public office. The rest of the inscription stresses the cunning behind the Catholic plot to supply James with a son so opportunely, and expresses the opinion that honest Britannia would never believe that a device like the Trojan Horse would be used! A second silver medal struck in Holland shows Ericthonius escaping from a basket, while two frightened women can be seen in the distance. Ericthonius, according to Greek mythology, was born without the aid of a mother, the medal implying that Queen Mary was barren. On the reverse is a drooping rose-bush, two of its roses representing the king and queen, and some distance away a sucker (the prince) is appearing from the earth. This drives home the medallist's point that the parentage of the baby is in doubt. The inscription 'tamen nascatur oportet' ('nevertheless it became necessary for him to be born'), suggests that James arranged a fictitious birth to strengthen his hold over his kingdom.

Naturally medals were struck joyfully proclaiming the genuine birth of a prince. Smeltzing struck a silver one at the orders of Ignatius White, Marquis d'Albeville, Ambassador Extraordinary for England in Holland, which shows on the reverse the queen in bed with her baby, with the inscription 'felicitas publica' ('the nation's joy'). Below this is a lengthy inscription giving the date of birth and details of White's ordering of the issue. The obverse has the bust of the king. Bower struck a silver medal, too, depicting the infant prince on a cushion with genii holding trumpets and a scroll inscribed 'Veniat centesimus haeres' ('The hundredth heir comes') on the reverse. Its obverse has the royal coat of arms and crown supported by genii, two of whom hold the shield of Cornwall and the prince's plume, together with an inscription giving his titles and date of birth.

A Dutch silver medal struck in 1688 became known as the Anti-Christian Confederacy Medal, for it proclaimed the rumour that a secret treaty had been made between James II and Louis XIV called the 'French league to cut Protestants' throats in England'. This rumour was linked with another that James had allowed Barbary pirates to carry captured Dutch ships to the port of Tangier, which then belonged to England, having been part of Catherine of Braganza's dowry. The obverse depicts James and Louis with Soliman III, the Moslem Caliph, and the Bey of Algiers, all of whom are confirming their alliance at a lighted altar bearing the symbols of their religions. On the reverse there are the three lilies of France supporting the crescent of Turkey, under a Jesuit's cap, sword and thunderbolt. The inscription 'In foedere quintus' ('A fifth in league'), refers to the devil, who is assisting the four rulers to overthrow Christianity in England.

WILLIAM OF ORANGE ARRIVES, JAMES DEPARTS

In spite of his impatience to acquire England, William of Orange sent his representative to England to congratulate James on the birth of his son; but when that representative returned to Holland he carried an invitation, bearing numerous signatures, requesting William to invade. These events are commemorated in a propaganda silver medal, probably struck by Smeltzing in 1688. The busts of

William and Mary appear on the obverse, while on the reverse the figure of Religion is resting one hand on a cap of liberty and a Bible, and holding a scroll in the other, while trampling on the emblems of popery. The scroll is inscribed 'Litterae Fagelii' ('Letter of Fagel'), and the Latin inscription translates 'Rome's angry pipe now takes a gentle tone. The Reformation of England 1688'. The reverse makes the point that the Protestants mistrust the Declarations of Indulgence which James has issued to support his cause.

For years William had known that his chances of becoming King of England were considerable, since he was the only male Protestant heir and had married his only real rival in 1677. He had had thousands of copies of propaganda leaflets prepared for distribution by secret agents when the time for invasion came, and his invading army's equipment included a printing press to produce his first proclamations as king, which he would validate with the seals bearing the arms of England he had made for the purpose. His invasion and its success was the subject of a number of medals.

Arondeaux struck a silver medal to commemorate William's landing at Torbay on Monday 5 November 1688. On the reverse, troops can be seen landing from rowing and sailing boats, the latter carrying a single sail. In the background is the fortified harbour wall of Torbay, with a Latin inscription, translating 'Against the child of Perdition. The naval expedition for the liberty of England 1688'. The 'child of Perdition' is the Pope. On the obverse are the figures of William (dressed as a Roman emperor) and Britannia (wearing the three crowns one on top of the other) shaking hands over a brazier that could be taken to be an altar. Behind Britannia is the shield of Britain hanging from intertwined orange and rose trees, while in the distance James II and his confessor, Father Petre, can be seen carrying away the prince, who is holding a windmill. The Latin inscription on the obverse translates 'God our Protector, Justice our companion'. The windmill featuring in this and other medals of the time implies that the prince's father was a miller. The medal was also struck in gold, and is rare today.

Jan Luder, a Dutch medallist of no great repute, produced a silver medal showing William standing on a cliff and superintending

Page 82, The Later Stuarts (VI)
(1) and (2) William III lands in England, 1688; (3) William III embarks
for England, 1688; (4) Destruction of Roman Catholic chapels, 1688;
(5) The Church restored, 1689.

the disembarkation of his troops. Beside him is a flag inscribed 'For thes religi and liberty'; it is said that the flag had been flown on the ship that had brought him. On the obverse is the bust of William in armour and cloak. G. Bower's invasion medal emphasised that William had not come as a conqueror but by invitation, as the Latin inscription on the reverse makes plain in translation: 'Your power does not seize the empire, but receives it'. William is shown on horseback at the head of his army, which is drawn up on the seashore; the fleet can be seen in the distance, while in the foreground Mars is supporting a fainting Justice. The obverse has the bust of William in armour.

As the hunchbacked, asthmatic William advanced steadily towards London, James put to sea in a ship which was found to be in need of ballast; when it put in for a load, the fishermen of Faversham seized and searched the king, not realising whom they had captured. He was brought back to London, and was still there when the advance guard of the Dutch army entered the Mall. Anxious not to have a captive king on his hands, William discreetly arranged for James to escape. The latter left at midday on Tuesday, 18 December, in the pouring rain, and four hours later William drove down Piccadilly.

James's flight is commemorated by a number of medals, of which Smeltzing's silver medal gives the most precise details. On the obverse is the bust of James, described in Latin as the fugitive king, while on the reverse is a column being shattered by lightning with a distant view of London behind it. A lengthy Latin inscription translates 'By no stroke of man but by God's breath. Willing fugitive on 20 December, captured 23 December 1688, and again a fugitive 2 January 1689'. The reason for the dating differing from that found in most textbooks is that England had not yet altered her calendar from the Julian to the Gregorian used on the Continent; thus by England's reckoning James was seized at Faversham on 13 December, returned to London on 16 December and finally left his capital on 18 December. The reference to God's breath presumably refers to the change of wind that had occurred on James's birthday, 14 October, enabling William to set sail for England. That day had been marked by an eclipse of the sun, and it was also the anniversary of the battle of Hastings, when another William had conquered England due to a change in the wind.

Smeltzing struck another silver medal to commemorate the flight; it has the same obverse as his first but the reverse shows a broken oak tree (James) and an orange tree (William), and behind them the sun is rising to show ships crossing the sea. The translation of the Latin inscription reads 'The government of the realm entrusted to the Prince of Orange after the flight of the king'. The linking of William's assumption of power with the flight of James was deliberately made to ease the consciences of those Englishmen who held to the theory of the divine right of kings, which rejected any idea that kingship was dependent on a 'contract' between king and people.

A more satirical medal was struck in lead by Wermuth, depicting a Belgic lion driving away James, who is holding a broken sword, and Father Petre, who has the windmill-clutching baby prince in his arms. The lion is driving them towards a French ship, which is waiting for them. The Latin inscription is blunt: 'Either king or nothing. James flees to Louis XIV'. The obverse carries the head of Louis XIV. Notice the appearance of the windmill again, implying that the prince's father was a miller. Another medal shows Father Petre mounted on a lobster, holding the prince, on whose head is a windmill, while behind them is a ship flying a French flag. The inscription is in French and consists of Petre's words of encouragement to the prince: 'Allons mon prince nous sommes en bon chemin'. The lobster refers to the story that the founder of the Jesuits dropped his Bible into the sea and was presented with it the next morning by a lobster. The reverse bears a shield showing a windmill surmounted by a Jesuit's cap and surrounded by a rosary with the inscription, 'Honi soit qui non y pense'; and also a lobster badge, with a French inscription reading, 'The arms and badge of the pretended Prince of Wales'.

Mauger struck a silver medal to commemorate Louis XIV's reception of the fugitive king, showing Louis' head on the obverse, and the figure of Gallia receiving James, his wife and his son on the reverse. The Latin inscription records their arrival in 1689. Smeltzing also struck another with the same obverse, but showing, on the reverse, the sun partially eclipsed by the moon above a scene of ships at sea. The sun represents Louis, here partially eclipsed by the fortunes of James, symbolised by the moon. A Latin inscription notes this and records Louis' reception of the fugitive king on 7 January 1689.

Meanwhile, on 10 December 1688, London had witnessed the burning of furniture from Roman Catholic chapels in Lincoln's Inn Fields, and Bower struck a silver medal to mark the occasion. The reverse shows a large bonfire in front of the west side of Lincoln's Inn Fields, where the Portuguese Catholic chapel in Duke Street can be seen in ruins; the Latin inscription speaks of 'just retribution'. The obverse has the busts of William and Mary, who are described as 'defenders of the faith', a title originally conferred on Henry VIII for his defence of the Catholic church, but later transferred to the defence of the Church of England.

Smeltzing commemorated the Commons' vote offering William and Mary the throne by a silver medal showing a bear (James), wearing a rosary, being stung by bees from three overturned hives (the three kingdoms). The sting represents the vote of the Commons, transferring the throne to a new occupant, and that no Roman Catholics are to hold any office. The Latin inscription points out that punishment follows crime, and continues by stating that English liberty and religion have been preserved. On the reverse the bear is wearing a Jesuit's cap in addition to the rosary, and is being driven by hands from heaven in the direction of the distant Sorbonne, and a lengthy Latin inscription emphasises that Britain is now free from the arbitrary power of the papacy. The importance of religious liberty is stressed on other medals dealt with below.

A duplicate coronation chair was made for the joint coronation of king and queen, since it was felt necessary to stress that they were of equal status. Normally a queen does not sign state documents, when there is a king also, but, as Mary's claim to the throne was stronger than William's, it was felt that by placing her on an equal footing William might prove more acceptable. A new coronation oath was used in which they promised to uphold 'the Protestant Reformed Religion established by law', and to rule by the law of the land. Naturally numerous medals were struck to celebrate the occasion.

George Bower made two gold coronation medals. The first has

the busts of William and Mary on the obverse and Perseus rescuing Andromeda (England) on the reverse; the second has the same obverse, but, on the reverse, two bishops supporting the crown over the heads of the king and queen, who are seated beneath a canopy and each holding a sceptre and orb. The Latin inscription translates 'Idolatry and slavery broken; religion, law and liberty restored'. This was the official medal, which was presented to those who took part in the ceremony.

The spectators at the coronation received a medal struck in gold, silver or lead, which has been attributed to Bower and more recently to Roettier. The obverse has the busts of William and Mary, while the reverse shows the earth in flames with Jupiter in the clouds hurling a thunderbolt at Phaeton (James), who is falling from his chariot (since he was unable to hold the reins of government). The inscription 'ne totus absumatur' ('that it may not all be consumed') suggests that James had been divinely displaced in order that the country might be saved from destruction. It is not very easy to find this medal today.

One of Jan Smeltzing's four silver coronation medals has the heads of William and Mary on the obverse. The reverse is very elaborate: an orange tree is intertwined with a rose and thistle, and bears the arms of Britain on a shield; on either side of the tree lightning is striking at James, who has dropped his crown and sceptre, and at Father Petre, who is carrying the baby prince; the latter clutches his windmill and a pyx. A lengthy Latin motto points out that, on the occasion of the coronation, tyranny and papacy have been expelled. Part of the inscription uses the words 'Ite missa est', which are used in the mass at the dismissal of the communicants near the end of the service; but here they refer to the dismissal of James and the Roman Catholics from England. Another of Smeltzing's medals has the same obverse; but its reverse has an eagle (William) casting a young bird (the baby prince) out of a nest in which two eaglets (Mary and Anne) remain, while the fleet can be seen in the distance under the midday sun.

An interesting silver medal, which has been attributed to Smeltzing, compares the success of the 1688 Revolution with the failure of Argyll's rebellion on behalf of the Duke of Monmouth. The reverse has a female figure of Fortune, with two heads, standing on the globe, through which a snake is slithering; one of the figure's heads is that of a boar (the Argyll crest), and her hand on that side is holding an axe and pointing to the Tower of London, which bears the date '1684'; her other head has a human face (William's) and her hand on that side holds a crown above Whitehall, which is dated '1689'. The inscription translates 'Another earned a traitor's death, but he a crown'. Argyll, as previously mentioned, was executed for his part in the Monmouth rebellion. The obverse has a Hydra defeating its enemy by the number of its heads, one of which, wearing a crown, is William's; the inscription translates 'Victorious by numbers, not by right'.

The position of the Church of England within the state was one of the basic points at issue in the 1688 Revolution, and at least two medals bear witness to this. A rare silver medal was struck by George Bower, with the busts of William and Mary on the obverse and William, dressed in Roman costume, holding the model of a church in one hand and a sword in the other while standing on a pedestal, on the reverse. At either end of the pedestal are two figures representing Time and History, who are recording William's career. The inscription on the pedestal is 'Aere perennius' ('More durable than brass'), and an inscription in the sky reads 'Caelo delabitur alto' ('He comes down from the lofty heaven'). The other medal was struck in silver by Philip Muller, who worked at Augsburg and Nuremberg; it commemorates the passing of the Toleration Act, and is a good example of how a medal can become over-crowded with symbolism, having little meaning at first glance. The obverse has the bust of William in armour and wearing a cloak, but the reverse has Britannia welcoming William while at the same time trampling on fires, chains and yokes, all of which are meant to symbolise superstition and tyranny. Britannia is attended by Religion holding a Cross and Bible, and Liberty holding a cornucopia, a scroll inscribed 'Test', and a staff with a cap of liberty. William is accompanied by a Belgic lion carrying a sheaf of arrows. Its two inscriptions translate 'Preserved by you we serve no lord. To the restorer of Britain, 1689'.

The importance of the Toleration Act is often only partially understood today. In 1689 two bills were introduced into Parliament —the Comprehension Bill, designed to offer generous terms for

Nonconformist clergy to return to the Church of England, and the Toleration Bill, to permit freedom of preaching and worship to the remaining few Nonconformists who did not accept the Comprehension Bill's terms. Unfortunately the first bill failed to pass, so when the second was passed Nonconformist clergy were obliged to apply for licences under its terms. Over 2,500 applied, and with them went their 500,000 followers, facing Archbishop Tenison with the difficult problem of reorganising the Church of England to cope with officially recognised rival churches. As the ecclesiastical courts dealt with cases concerning marriage, probate, adultery and bastardy, among many others, the effect of the Toleration Act was to remove many people from the jurisdiction of the only civil courts that could solve their problems. Societies for the reform of manners now had to tackle the drift to permissiveness that followed, while a new High Church party under Bishop Atterbury of Rochester tried in vain to re-establish a one-church state. Thus, whether William III, as hailed by Bower's medal, was the restorer of the national church or not is rather a debatable point.

IRELAND

James II's landing at Kinsale in Ireland in March 1689 marked the beginning of a lengthy Irish campaign. J. Boskam struck a silver medal to commemorate the relief of Londonderry after its 105-day siege by Jacobites. The obverse has the bust of William on a pedestal, Minerva and Plenty crowning him, while in the distance is a view of Londonderry with ships sailing to its relief. The Latin inscription proclaims William as its liberator. On the reverse the bust of Louis XIV is being crowned by Gallia and Germany, while the two towns (Mayence and Bonn) can be seen under siege in the distance. The reverse commemorates Louis' loss of those cities in 1689. The Rev George Walker led the 7,000 besieged people of Londonderry and his chief concern was the shortage of food; horseflesh went up to 8½p (1s 8d) per lb and a quarter of a dog cost 27½p (5s 6d). One fat man hid himself for three days for fear of being eaten. James's army only consisted of some 6,000 men— who had thirty shovels to help them undermine the town's walls. In a later century the great Napoleon maintained that one needed four times as many men outside a town as there were in it, if a siege was to be successful, so it is difficult to see why Walker allowed himself to be shut up for so long. A squadron of three relief ships arrived in July and broke the enemy's boom across the River Foyle. The first ship to hit the boom rebounded and ran aground, but was refloated by the propelling force of its guns when a broadside was fired!

In those days it was customary to hire foreign mercenaries when extra forces were needed, and William's hiring of 6,000 foot and 1,000 horse from Christian V of Denmark on 25 August 1689 is commemorated by a silver medal struck by Barthold Meier, chief Danish medallist. The obverse shows a fleet at sea, and the reverse is covered with an inscription, translating 'Christian V sends William III 7,000 soldiers, 1689'. The need for William's presence in Ireland is commemorated by a silver medal struck by Jan Luder, a relatively unimportant Dutch medallist. The obverse depicts William in armour and cloak, with an inscription giving his titles and stating that Luder made the medal. On the reverse Neptune can be seen rising from the sea, and Ireland, with a nymph on a rock, begging Jupiter to overthrow Phaeton, the son of the Sun-god and famous for his bad driving of his father's chariot. The inscription translates 'If not you, who will put out the fires?' As a result of earnest petitions, William left London for Ireland on 4 June 1690. His departure is recalled by Smeltzing's silver medal showing his bust on the obverse, and an eagle flying towards land, bearing olive and orange branches and a sceptre, with the fleet approaching the shore, on the reverse. The inscription records the date of his departure.

William's depature meant that the Queen had to be made regent, an action performed by Parliament on 7 May 1690 and commemorated in the form of silver and copper medals struck by Johann Crocker, or Croker, who was born in Dresden, worked in Holland and then came to England. As a result of his work in William's reign he was made Chief Engraver at the Mint in 1704 and kept the post until his death in 1741. His medal has the bust of the Queen on the obverse and the full moon shining on a landscape on the reverse. It is inscribed 'Ex nocte diem' ('From night, day'). She was faced with the consequences of a naval action off Beachy Head while William was away, when the French succeeded in bringing their Toulon fleet into the Channel to join the fleet already there and turn on the combined Dutch and English fleets under the Earl of Torrington. The Earl considered his fifty-six ships were no match for the sixty-eight ships of the enemy and advised the queen against risking a battle; but the government ordered him to attack and the resulting action was known as the battle of Beachy Head (30 June 1690). Torrington deliberately let the Dutch ships take the brunt of the battle, with the result that they lost four ships and the English only one, and the French were victorious. William promised the angry Dutch that Torrington should be court-martialled, and, though acquitted, the admiral was never given a command again.

Two silver medals (among a number of others), both by Smeltzing, commemorated the action. The first has the heads of William and Mary on the obverse; and, on the reverse, Mary, wearing her crown and holding a trident and cornucopia, is looking at ships undergoing repair in the distance, while a prisoner (Lord Torrington) is being conducted to the Tower of London. The Latin inscription recalls that the regent queen rebuilt the defeated navy. The second medal has the bust of Louis XIV wearing cloak and armour, and is inscribed 'Invictissimus Ludovicus Magnus' ('The unconquered Louis the Great'). The reverse shows him as Neptune, driving over the sea brandishing a trident, while a naval battle is going on in the background. The Latin inscription translates 'Fly with all speed, he [Louis] rules the sea', and is addressed to the English and Dutch. Smeltzing was now working in the Paris mint, since his satirical medals of William had forced him to leave Holland.

The action off Beachy Head was not followed up by the French, one reason being that on the following day, 11 July, William won the battle of the River Boyne, when his 33,000 men forded the river and defeated James's 21,000. Three not particularly good medals commemorated the victory, Jan Luder striking two of them in silver. Both depict William in armour and cloak on the obverse, and, as with all Luder's medals, record the maker's name ('Jan Luder fecit'). The reverse has Bellona, goddess of war, with spear and shield, watching the battle from a distance—William's cavalry are pursuing the enemy towards a city marked 'Dublins'. His second medal has the king on horseback commanding the battle, which is to be seen in the background. James and Lausun, commander of the French auxiliaries, are fleeing, while George Walker lies dead in the middle of the fight and Marshal Schomberg, William's general, lies dead on another part of the field. The Latin inscription translates 'His appearance scattered the enemy'. It was Lausun who advised James to flee when the battle turned against them. The third commemorative medal was struck in silver by Arondeaux, and depicts the bust of William in armour and cloak on the obverse, and William on horseback fording the river at the head of his cavalry, with the enemy fleeing, on the reverse. The inscription translates 'Scornful of wounds and all that bars his way, he ejected James and rebuilt Ireland'.

Luder was responsible for a silver medal commemorating William's triumphal entry into Dublin on 16 July 1690. The obverse is the same as the reverse of his medal depicting the deaths of Walker and Schomberg, mentioned above. The reverse has the king presenting a cap of liberty to the figure of Ireland, while James can be seen fleeing in the distance. The Latin inscription translates 'He preserves their homes and families, and triumphantly enters Dublin after driving out the French and rebels [Irish]'. This denunciation of the Irish as rebels gave great offence even to William's supporters. It was Smeltzing who was responsible for the silver medal marking James's flight from Ireland to France later in 1690. The obverse has the bust of James, with a Latin inscription describing him as a fugitive king, while the reverse has a stag with winged feet running and looking over its shoulder, with an inscription from Virgil's *Aeneid* (viii, 224), 'Pedibus timor addidit alas' ('Fear added wings to his feet'), together with the date, 12 July.

The following year, 1691, William left Mary as regent again while he went to Holland for a triumphal visit. Smeltzing commemorated Mary's regency with a silver medal depicting William and Mary on the obverse, and a lioness trampling on snakes near a cave occupied by three cubs, while the lion departs, on the reverse. The lion and lioness are the king and queen and the cubs the three kingdoms of England, Scotland and Ireland. William's arrival at the Hague was marked by the issuing of a silver medal by D. Koene, which shows the king and his suite pulling to the shore in an open boat with a man on horseback riding into the water towards them. The Latin inscription asks the horseman what he fears, since he has ridden into the water, suspicious about the approaching boat. Beneath the picture the inscription continues by pointing out that William has returned through ice, storms and quicksands (his passage is known to have been a particularly stormy one). The reverse shows something of the rejoicing that followed his return; fireworks and a triumphal arch can be seen.

Rebellion in Ireland broke out again in 1691 and on 22 July General Ginckel attacked and defeated the Irish and French troops under St Ruth near the castle of Aughrim, and this battle was marked by the issue, among others, of a silver medal by Jan Smeltzing, with the king and queen on the obverse, and a battle scene depicting cavalry in action on the reverse. This battle has been claimed to be the greatest pitched battle in Irish history for both armies numbered some 20,000. In the same year Ginckel, a Dutchman, successfully besieged Athlone, Galway and Sligo, feats which are recorded on another of Smeltzing's silver medals. The obverse has the busts of William and Mary, while the reverse shows the shield of Ireland and three medallions with the names and surrender dates of the three cities. In each case double dates are given because of the difference between the English and Dutch calendars.

The treaty of Limerick, signed in 1691, was the subject of numerous medals. By this treaty Roman Catholics were allowed to retain the privileges they had enjoyed in the reign of Charles II, but they could not vote, be parliamentary candidates or join the army. The treaty allowed Catholic soldiers to go to France if they wished and some 10,000 did so, and there they formed an Irish brigade in the French army. Marlborough found them facing him at the battle of Blenheim.

IN SEARCH OF WEALTH

With affairs in Ireland settled, it is possible to pause for a moment and consider three events marked by medals before continuing the saga of William's military career. The first was the conclusion of a long attempt to salvage a Spanish ship in the West Indies off Hispaniola. As early as the reign of Charles II, Captain William

Phipps had attempted to recover the treasure aboard the ship, which had sunk some forty-four years earlier. He was unsuccessful and nearly had to abandon his efforts due to lack of money soon after James II came to the thone. However, the Duke of Albemarle and some of his friends advanced the necessary funds and he finally succeeded in bringing home silver treasure worth £300,000. Bower struck gold and silver medals for those who took part and other courtiers. On the obverse are the busts of James II and Mary, for the medal was struck in 1687 and the bulk of the rescue work was in their reign. On the reverse is a ship, whose boats are engaged in fishing up treasure from the wreck. The Latin legend comes from Ovid (*Art Am*, iii, 425) and translates 'Always let your hook be hanging'. Below are the words 'Naufraga reperta, 1687' ('Wreck recovered, 1687').

In 1694 a copper medal was struck with what might be taken as an ominous warning note on its obverse—'God preserve Carolina and the Lords Proprietors, 1694'. The reverse has an elephant with large tusks. Carolina had originally been intended as a single colony, but separate expeditions led to it becoming two. The Lords Proprietors were the owners of the colonies who had received their grant from Charles II. The intention had been to supply England with silks, wines, fruits and oils, but this had not worked out, the northern colony turning to illicit trading to break the Navigation Acts, and the southern taking up rice-growing, with slave labour, one overseer looking after thirty slaves. The struggles between James II and William III in England were of concern to the colonists, for the victor might alter the laws governing trade and influence their forms of religious worship. Carolina felt that 1694 was a time when God's help was needed, hence the medal.

An extremely rare silver-gilt medal was struck in 1700 by Martin Smeltzing, the younger brother of Jan, to celebrate a temporary victory of the Scots over the Spaniards in the Scottish colony of New Caledonia on the Darien Isthmus. The obverse has a High-lander dressed in armour, bearing a shield decorated with a unicorn, and holding his sword in his hand as he advances towards a fort that is being stormed in the background. The Latin inscription translates 'What not for one's country. At Toubucan, where

Captain Alexander Campbell put to flight 1,600 Spaniards, 8 Feb. 1700'. On the reverse is the coat of arms of the African & Indian Company of Scotland, with helmet, crest and supporters, and an inscription which translates 'To wherever the world extends. Power stronger by union'.

Behind this medal lies an extraordinary story. Scotland had long envied the prosperity England seemed to derive from her colonies and some Scotsmen decided that they should try and imitate her. They formed a company which was originally designed to trade in Africa and the West and East Indies, but William Patterson suggested that they would do better if they started a colony at Darien, near Panama, and produced a manuscript called *Wafer's Journal*, in which a surgeon called Wafer described the area he had visited when working for the explorer Dampier. They secretly sent to England for Wafer, who crossed the border into Scotland at night, using the name 'Mr Brown'. He convinced them that Darien would be ideal, and so an expedition was prepared, though its precise destination was kept secret. Money poured in from all kinds of people and apothecaries were ordered to prepare enough medicines for 1,500 colonists for two years. Gunsmiths were told to make pistols at 85p (17s) or 90p (18s) a pair, and 'a bargain of bibles and catechisms' was purchased from a printer's widow for £50. The expedition finally set out in July 1698, but it soon ran into trouble, for not only were the provisions found to be made of 'damnified wheat', but English colonists and ships refused to help; the Indians in Darien were friendly but not the nearby Spaniards; and the hoped-for gold turned out to be valueless. The Scots sent encouraging reports home, however, but a few weeks later abandoned the settlement.

Two further expeditions left Scotland, the second with 1,300 settlers, and each in turn arrived to find the settlement abandoned as each effort collapsed. Although the medal records one successful attack on the Spaniards, the colonists finally lost the struggle, the enterprise costing Scotland some 2,000 lives and £200,000. Faced with heavy debts the nation eventually bowed to the Act of Union (1707) with England by which the company was closed down and Scotland received £398,085 towards her economy in exchange for her independence.

WARS AND TREATIES

William III's military career continued with a war known by four names—the War of the League of Augsburg, the War of the Grand Alliance, the King's War or the War of the English Succession. The last two titles present different English attitudes towards the war, for it was regarded by some as King William's personal war for the sake of Holland, and by others as the war that would settle the succession to the English throne.

It was the subject of many commemorative medals, which naturally served for propaganda, one such celebrating the battle of La Hogue, fought 19–24 May 1692. Ninety ships of the English and Dutch fleets, commanded by Admirals Russell and Almonde, faced fifty French ships under Admiral Tourville. The French admiral fought in a disadvantageous position close in to his own shore, and in spite of his good leadership lost fifteen ships of the line in the deep water of the bay of La Hogue, with the result that the French navy did not recover for the rest of the war.

A large silver medal was struck by Philipp Muller, a native of Augsburg. On the obverse William III is seen dressed as a Roman and holding a rudder, with Hibernia holding her harp and Belgium with cap of liberty and her lion beside him. Victory hovers above and crowns William with a laurel wreath. On the reverse the naval battle can be seen in full action, the signs of the Zodiac cutting across the sky so that the sun is shown leaving Gemini and passing towards Cancer, Leo and Virgo; the inscription, 'Solis iter' ('the course of the sun') emphasises that the sun's position dates the battle. Below the action an inscription records the date and claims a great victory. The edge of this medal was lettered by F. Kleinert, who employed Muller at Nuremberg, and it is an interesting example of chronogrammatic art, though it takes some working out. It reads 'ConCastIgatVs gaLLorVM eastVs et astVs fLVCtIbVs, et pVgna fraCtVs atroCe fragor' ('The pride and cunning of the French on the sea chastised and the crash effected by a severe contest'). The capitals make CCIVLLVMVVLVCIV-VCVC, which can be rewritten MCCCCCLLLVVVVVVVII, or MDCXCII, hence 1692.

R. Arondeaux produced one gold and two silver medals on this occasion. The gold has the busts of William and Mary on the obverse, and the naval action on the reverse. The latter is partly concealed and spoilt by a seated warrior holding a trident surmounted by a wreath, and leaning on a shield bearing united hands; the warrior is seated on a lion and unicorn, which represent the two allied admirals, and the shield of France is lying at his feet. One of Arondeaux's silver medals has Admirals Russell and Almonde riding in a sea-chariot inscribed with their names; one of them is holding a trident with a broom attached to it, the other a sword, and the naval action can be seen in the distance, with Louis XIV (with a trident) escaping on a sea-shell drawn by frogs. The Latin inscription translates 'Sweeping the false Neptune (Louis) from the sea'. The reverse is the same as the reverse of his gold medal. Arondeaux's second silver medal has a similar picture to that on the obverse of his first, except that Louis is dropping his trident, but the reverse shows the blowing up of the French flagship *Le Soleil Royal*, on whose stern can be seen Louis' emblem of the Sun and his motto 'Nec pluribus impar' ('no poor match for many a foe'); this motto is parodied by the inscription 'Nunc pluribus impar' ('a poor match now for many a foe'). The ship, at the time regarded as the finest warship in Europe, had to be run ashore at Cherbourg, where it was later burnt to the waterline, by Admiral Delaval.

J. Boskam's silver medal shows better workmanship than Arondeaux's medals, and at the same time gives a more vigorous treatment of the battle scene. Its reverse shows the naval action, with a sinking ship and clouds of smoke, while in the foreground a lion and unicorn are to be seen racing after a French cock, though the unicorn is hampered by a trident it is carrying in the crook of its foreleg. There is a Latin inscription to the effect that we are now masters of the sea and the French fleet has been destroyed. The obverse has the bust of William III in armour and cloak. The claim for mastery of the sea is a retort to Louis' similar claim after the battle of Beachy Head in 1690.

The war in the Netherlands was a slow war of sieges, since it was determined by the river system and the line of French forts and not by decisive pitched battles. Through 1692 and 1693 the French were steadily successful and marked their success with the issue of commemorative medals. For example, a silver medal was issued to celebrate the taking on Namur on 30 June 1692. It shows Louis riding on horseback, accompanied by his staff, to receive the surrender of the garrison, while in the distance the Allied army is visible. Unfortunately, William had arrived with 100,000 men just too late to relieve the city. Later in the same year a medal was struck in copper by Joseph Roettier and Molart to commemorate the battle of Steinkirk on 3 August. William had hoped to surprise the French but his plan went wrong when Count Solmes failed to support the English troops, and the Allies retreated after losing 7,000 men. The obverse of this medal has the bust of Louis XIV, and the reverse the picture of a French soldier striking a prostrate enemy whom he is holding by his cravat.

England's first reply in this publicity war was a silver medal by Boskam to mark the execution of Captain Grandval, a French dragoon, who had been sent by James II and Louis to enter the Allied camp and assassinate William. The medal's obverse has the bust of William, laureated, armoured and cloaked, with a Latin inscription claiming that he was unconquerable. The reverse depicts a monument on which the executioner can be seen giving the 'coup de grace' to Grandval; on either side are poles and gallows with the quarters and head of the offender, and a Latin inscription records his name and crime. Boskam marked William's checking of the French advance at Landen in 1693 with a medal showing a falcon pouncing upon a heron, while a battle near towns can be seen behind them.

The issuing of propaganda medals continued throughout 1694. A French silver medal by J. Mauger marked the failure of Admiral the Earl of Berkeley and General Talmash to lead an expedition to Brest. It has been argued in the past that Marlborough and the leading politician Godolphin had betrayed the plan to James II; certainly they had come to believe that a Jacobite restoration was possible and that they and others could stomach William no longer, but the letter Marlborough is supposed to have written to James about the expedition is probably a forgery. Mauger's medal has the head of Louis on the obverse with a Latin inscription declaring him to be a great and most Christian king. The reverse has the figure of Minerva, armed and facing the seashore, with an inscription concerning the guarding of the coastline.

Page 98, The Later Stuarts (VII)
(1) Fortunes of Rebellion, 1689; (2) Battle of Dunkirk, 1695; (3) Plot to assassinate William III, 1696; (4) Battle of the Boyne, 1690; (5) Darien Expedition, 1700.

Boskam supplied the English medals for 1694, starting with two and, later, using their reverses to form a third. One of his silver medals commemorates the visit of the Prince of Baden to England in January, the obverse showing William receiving the Prince at his palace gates, with the figure of Silence seated near the shields of Germany and England, surmounted by a cap of liberty. The Prince had been sent by the Emperor of Germany to discuss possible action against Louis XIV. The reverse marked the bombardment of Dieppe in July by the combined English and Dutch fleets, and shows Neptune riding in his sea-chariot before that town, which is under fire from the fleet. Another of Boskam's silver medals marked the bombardment of Havre by the same fleet between 26 and 28 July. Boskam emphasised that this and other bombardments were in retaliation for similar French actions by the design on the reverse of his medal, which shows the Bull of Perillus being heated over flames while the battle of Havre rages in the background. Perillus had been destroyed by the brazen bull he had invented in order to burn the victims of Phalaris, the tyrant of Agrigentum; the Latin inscription can be freely translated 'Hoisted by their own petard'. A gold medal was struck to mark the bombardment of Dunkirk and other towns by the English fleet under Sir Cloudesley Shovel in September; the obverse has William in Roman dress holding a thunderbolt, while the reverse shows ships bombarding towns along the coast.

In 1695 Boskam was faced with the task of striking medals to mourn the death of Queen Mary on 7 January. He produced three, all silver, bearing a portrait of the queen on their obverses but having different reverses. One shows a monument on which are seated the three Fates, decorated with a medallion of the Queen and reliefs representing the funeral procession. Another has a monument consisting of two small obelisks flanking a larger one, decorated with a medallion of the queen. The third is symbolic, depicting the queen as a unicorn, the symbol of purity, which has purified the earth by killing a snake, scorpion and toads, and is in the act of leaping up into the sky. The symbolism has been criticised as grotesque. The Latin inscription states that she is 'snatched from our sight, but first she destroyed our plagues', and continues 'Mary, the delight and comfort of the British world, lamented'.

The war continued and Mauger on Louis' behalf struck a silver medal to mark the unsuccessful attempt of the English and Dutch fleets to bombard Dunkirk in August. The reverse shows the bombardment and a ship sinking, with a Latin inscription claiming that the city was undamaged; the obverse has the bust of Louis. Boskam's opportunity to retaliate came in September, when William achieved one of his greatest victories, the recapture of Namur after it had been provided with the most modern system of fortification. The obverse has the bust of the king, and the reverse shows him on horseback commanding his forces at the siege, which lasted three months. The Latin inscription records that it was stormed 'in view of a helpless force of 100,000 men', referring to the belated arrival of a French relieving force; it is interesting to note that William had lost it earlier in similar circumstances. Joy at William's success being so great, it is understandable that a gold medal was also struck showing the king radiant like a sun, galloping along near the city on the obverse, and the figure of Fame flying across the reverse, carrying a trumpet with the arms of William on its flag; the motto reads 'William III, the greatest'.

A lull in the fighting in 1696, which preceded the peace treaty in 1697, meant that the medallists had no military events of any great importance to record, but there was a serious assassination attempt against William. The temptation to assassinate William had increased, since his death would leave no Queen Mary on the throne. In February James II moved to Calais, which was the signal for great activity by Jacobite agents. It was decided that Sir George Barclay should lead some forty men in an attack on William as he drove home to Kensington Palace from his weekly hunting trip in Richmond Park, the attack to take place when he was passing through a narrow muddy lane between the River Thames and Turnham Green. It was fixed for 3 March, but some of the conspirators talked too much and William heard the details, the Habeas Corpus Act was suspended and eventually eight conspirators were executed.

Boskam's silver medal has the bust of William, laurel-crowned and armed with a shield inscribed in Hebrew with the name of Yahweh—who, according to a Latin motto, is protecting the king.

The reverse shows six figures holding daggers, torches and snakes, restrained by cords from heaven. Another silver medal has the heads of Louis XIV and James II on the obverse, with an inscription labelling them as Herod and Pilate. The reverse shows an enclosure wherein Louis and James are holding purse and daggers, Father Petre a pyx, and the young prince is riding a Jesuit lobster; outside the enclosure the conspirators can be seen in a wood marked '40', while in the distance there is a fleet. The inscription refers to *Genesis* 49, v 5–6, in which Simeon and Levi are plotting. This medal is of poor quality and the effort at satire weak and clumsy.

There were two subjects for medallists in 1697, the treaty of Ryswick and propaganda for James II's cause. The treaty was signed by England, Holland, Spain and France on 30 September and the Empire signed it on 31 October. Numerous medals were struck to mark the occasion, though none are particularly outstanding. Boskam produced several, one of which has a pleasant view of the Palace of Ryswick on the reverse, with the Latin inscription 'Pax Huic Domui' ('Peace be to this house'); the obverse shows the Belgic lion wearing a crown and holding an olive branch, sword and scales while resting on a globe, and carries a Latin inscription claiming that equity is the outcome of this peace. Boskam produced a second silver medal, with the head of William on the obverse, and four right hands coming out of clouds to unite in the form of a cross; while a third medal of his shows corn growing in a helmet, which is now being used for peaceful purposes.

One of the key clauses of the Treaty of Ryswick was France's recognition of William as King of England, which led James II and his son, the Old Pretender, to retaliate with propaganda medals designed by N. Roettier. It is noticeable that a number of them were struck in copper-gilt and copper so that they could be widely distributed. Most of them concentrate on presenting the Old Pretender as Prince of Wales rather than reminding people that James II was still alive. The first has the bust of the Old Pretender dressed in armour and wearing a cloak, and is inscribed 'Jacobus Walliae Princeps' ('James, Prince of Wales') on the obverse; while the reverse has a ship flying the flag of England in distress, with a Latin inscription stating that he is thrown up, and not drowned, by the waves. A second medal has the head of the prince on the obverse and a dove with an olive branch flying over a tranquil sea, with an inscription claiming that he brings peace on the reverse. A third has the same obverse, but shows a mine exploding in a bastion on the reverse, which suggests that the Jacobite cause will overcome its enemies by force. It is interesting to note that one medal offers peace and the other violence. Two years later, in 1699, Roettier struck a silver medal with the head of James II on the obverse and that of the Prince on the reverse.

QUEEN ANNE

William III died in 1702 and the last Stuart monarch, Anne, succeeded him. Boskam's silver memorial medal shows the bust of the king in armour and cloak, with an eagle flying at sunset back to the mountains whence it had come and an inscription which translates 'Not till sunset wings he home' on the reverse. Unfortunately Boskam seems to have lacked the ability to draw an eagle in flight, and this spoils what otherwise would have been a good medal! M. Smeltzing also likened William to an eagle on his silver medal, which shows the bird flying from the temple of Janus and is inscribed with the date of his death, 19 March. The best of the memorial medals was that produced by J. Croker who became Chief Engraver at the Mint in Queen Anne's reign. Made of gold, it is cast and chased on the obverse and engraved on the reverse, and carries a ring for suspension. The obverse bears the bust of William, laureated, armoured and cloaked, in a dignified pose much superior to the usual pseudo-classical arrangement. Around the edge are the words 'In piam memoriam Gulielmi Regis 3' ('In pious memory of King William III'). The reverse has a crowned harp surrounded by a border of arms, flags, etc.

The accession of Queen Anne, whose mind has been described as moving as slowly as a lowland river, was hailed as a postponement of the evil day when the choice between Stuarts and Hanoverians had to be made. Her weight was legendary and a lifting apparatus had to be used to get her upstairs; and once it took twelve men to stop her coach rolling back down a hill in Bath when the horses could not hold it. Stories are told of her going hunting in a one-horse high-wheeled chaise, driving it furiously across cornfields, while ladies-in-waiting were tossed out of similar chaises all around her. Her accession on 8 March 1702 was marked by the striking of medals by Boskam and Croker. A silver medal of Croker's shows the bust of the queen, crowned and wearing the insignia of the Order of the Garter, on the obverse, and a statue showing Anne as Pallas Athene (Minerva), armed with spear and shield, on the reverse. That Latin inscription proclaims her as the new Pallas, a reference to the promise she made to the States General that she would assist Holland in resisting the encroachments of France. One medal struck in both gold and silver has been attributed by some to Boskam and by others to Croker. It shows the bust of the queen crowned and draped on the obverse; and, on the reverse, a heart surmounted by a crown within branches of laurel and oak and resting on a pedestal, and the inscription 'Entirely English'. These two words come from her speech to parliament, in which she said:

> As I know my own heart to be entirely English, I can sincerely assure you there is not anything you can expect or desire from me which I shall not be ready to do for the happiness and prosperity of England.

Her coronation medal has also been attributed to both Boskam and Croker in recent years. Struck in gold, silver and copper, it depicts the draped portrait of the queen on the obverse, and, on the reverse, Pallas (Anne) hurling a thunderbolt at a double-headed four-armed monster (France and Spain) which is holding clubs and stones, and whose lower limbs terminate in snakes. The Latin inscription translates 'She is the vice-regent of the thunderer'. In her address to her Council she had already stressed the need to prepare for war with France. The medal was struck for distribution among those present at the coronation, and the silver and copper versions are reasonably common today. The workmanship is not particularly good, however.

MARLBOROUGH'S CAMPAIGNS

The practice of striking medals to commemorate battles, which had become common during the reign of William III, was to continue in the new reign. In The War of the Spanish Succession, which occupied most of Anne's reign, the Duke of Marlborough was to make his name not only for his skill as a general but also for his care of his troops and for the introduction of new weapons.

He saw to it that medical attention was given to troops at the height of a battle instead of at its conclusion. He changed the role of the infantry from defence to aggression by introducing the flintlock and ring-bayonet, the latter enabling them to dispense with pikemen. He drilled his men in platoons instead of in ranks, which made them more mobile and allowed them to change the direction of fire.

Boskam recorded the opening of the fighting in the new reign when he issued a silver medal to mark the capitulation of the towns of Kaiserwerth, Venloo, Ruremonde, Stevenswart and Liége to Marlborough. The obverse has the crowned bust of the queen and the reverse shows Liége under bombardment, with an inscription listing the places taken. In the autumn of 1702 the combined English and Dutch fleets under Sir George Rooke attacked and destroyed the French and Spanish fleets in Vigo Bay. A silver medal by G. F. Nurnberger, who lived in Nuremberg, has a well designed view of the entry of the Allied fleets into Vigo harbour; fortifications and troops can be seen on land. A reference in the Latin inscription to favourable winds refers to the breaking of the boom at the harbour entrance by Hobson's ship, the *Torbay*. On the obverse Neptune can be seen, in his sea-chariot, and Victory is holding a scroll inscribed with the names of French and Spanish ships taken or destroyed; below this scene are three sea-genii holding the shields of England, Germany and Holland. The gold and silver coins struck from the bullion captured by this raid have the inscription 'Vico' under the bust of the queen. Boskam's medal of the event shows the fleets fighting it out in the bay, whereas Nurnberger's medal shows the Allied fleet as it enters to start the attack.

In 1704 Croker struck a 'Victories at Sea' medal which was sold to the public at £6. 6. o (£6.30) (gold), 7s (35p) (silver) and 2s 6d (12½p) (copper). On the obverse is a portrait of Queen Anne, while on the reverse Neptune in his sea-chariot is presenting a trident with crown and a mural crown to Britannia, who is seated on a rock, with the inscription 'Victoriae Navales' ('Naval victories'). The victories referred to were the capture of Gibraltar on 3 August and the action off Malaga on 24 August. The obvious advantages of securing Gibraltar as a naval base had led to the sending of the expedition, which had a relatively easy task, since the garrison

Page 105, The Later Stuarts (VIII)
(1) Battle of Blenheim, 1704; (2) Queen Anne's Bounty, 1704; (3) Siege of Tournay, 1709; (4) and (5) Castor and Pollux and the Battle of Oudenarde, 1708.

numbered only 470 and the new fortifications, which had been recently designed, were still in the early stages of construction. The action off Malaga was severe, however, but Sir George Rooke succeeded in defeating the French Toulon and Brest fleets.

The battle of Blenheim, fought on 13 August 1704, was clearly a subject made for medallists. Boskam produced a silver one, with a view of the battlefield showing Marlborough on horseback on the reverse, and the queen on the obverse. A silver medal by Christian Wermuth, a native of Altenburg, depicts the battle, with Prince Eugene and Marlborough driving the enemy into the Danube and Marshal Tallard surrendering his sword, under the figure of Fame, which is blowing two trumpets. The obverse has the busts of Prince Eugene and Marlborough. Marlborough's victory at Blenheim is too well known to be described further, though it is interesting to note his care for his troops in having seventeen doctors present on the battlefield, many more than usual. The cost of this care worked out at about twopence per man per month, which was deducted from their pay; there was also an insurance scheme of a farthing a day for hospital charges. The booty taken led to the issuing of bounties to the troops, privates drawing £1, colonels £120, and Marlborough £717.

It was on 3 November 1704 that Queen Anne restored the revenues from first-fruits and tithes, which had been appropriated to the Crown by Henry VIII, to the Church of England in order to establish a fund known as Queen Anne's Bounty, to raise the salaries of poor parsons and erect vicarages. The event was marked by gold and silver medals, struck by J. Croker, which have the bust of the queen on the obverse, and show her seated on a throne presenting a charter to kneeling bishops on the reverse. The Latin inscription records the details of the event.

Although 1705 was a disappointing year for Marlborough, he was depicted on a silver medal of Boskam's breaking through the French lines at Neerhespen on 17 July 1708. He is in the foreground of the battle scene, riding a horse, and on the obverse there is a bust of the queen. But the medal that marks the most important military gain of the year is Boskam's silver medal recording the capitulation of Barcelona to the Earl of Peterborough, accompanied by the Archduke Charles, who was asserting his claim to be Charles III of Spain. The obverse shows the bust of Charles, laureated and in armour and cloak, wearing the order of the Golden Fleece; the Latin inscription announces him as Charles III of Spain. The reverse shows Barcelona being bombarded by sea and land.

Barcelona's city walls were strong and the citadel of Montjuich on a 700 ft hill was regarded as impregnable by Peterborough's officers, though they did agree to an attempted siege for eighteen days. The Earl in his capacity as general pressed for the siege at council meetings of military officers, but as admiral rejected the plan when holding naval council meetings! After making preparations for retreat, he decided to trick the enemy by a feint, followed by a surprise attack. Splitting his men into three groups, he led the attack in the early hours of 14 September; initial success was followed by near disaster when his men panicked, but he checked them by a display of 'the horriblest passion that ever man was seen in'. Success came when they exploded the magazine, which they had rightly guessed was in the citadel's chapel. A few weeks later Charles was proclaimed King of Spain in Barcelona, and the whole of Valencia and Catalonia were taken. In the following year, 1706, the Earl and the King of Spain joined forces with the Earl of Galway, who had advanced from Portugal, and their combined strength led to Philip V's flight from Madrid on 11 May. This event was recorded by a silver medal issued by Kleinert and Lauffer in Nuremberg. On the obverse Philip is seen on horseback, dropping his crown and flying before Genius, who is covering the sun with the shield of Austria. The reverse reflects the success of Marlborough's campaign for that year, showing him on horseback galloping forward over fallen enemies, while women, representing fallen cities, surrender keys.

The battle of Ramillies was Marlborough's great success of 1706. Moving through dense fog in the early hours of Whit Sunday morning his scouts located the enemy dressed in the new uniforms which Louis had ordered for them. In the fury of the battle that followed Marlborough found himself surrounded and afoot when his horse threw him as it tried to clear a hedge. A colonel offered him his own horse, and, as Marlborough mounted it, a cannon ball removed the colonel's head from his shoulders. Marlborough later took care of his widow and children and erected a monument to him in Westminster Abbey. By late afternoon the enemy were retreating in chaos. Numerous medals were struck to commemorate the event. J. Croker's silver medal has the bust of Queen Anne on the obverse, and a map of the Low Countries, showing the areas which Marlborough had captured, supported by two winged Victories. Georg Hautsch, who worked in Cologne and Holland, struck a medal in both silver and pewter. The obverse has a fairly good portrait of Marlborough—three-quarter length with a full-bottomed wig, lace cravat, armour and the insignia of the Garter. The inscription in abbreviations of single letters proclaims him 'Prince of the Holy Roman Empire, Duke of Marlborough, Captain-General of the English Army'. On the reverse, Mars can be seen striding through dead and dying, holding a collection of trophies which include the shields of Brabant, Flanders and Antwerp. A Latin inscription records these events, while round the edge is a legend translating as 'Fierce in battle and ignorant of defeat in arms. Virgil'. (Hautsch is mistaken in attributing this saying to Virgil, for in fact it comes from Ovid, *Epist* II, ix, 45.)

The victories of Anne's forces over Louis XIV in 1706 are summed up on a Dutch silver medal by an unknown artist, whose theme is a king's defeat by a queen. On the obverse Anne is shown as Pallas Athene overthrowing Louis, who is dressed as a Roman warrior. The Latin inscription translates 'Louis the great, Anne the greater'. The reverse shows Abimelech (Louis) being struck by a millstone thrown by a woman (Anne) from the top of a tower which he is besieging; a lengthy inscription from *Judges* IX refers to the story of a woman killing Abimelech. On 11 July Marlborough and Prince Eugene won the battle of Oudenarde, so opening the road to Paris. Although the Allied victory owed much to the enemy's mistakes, there is no doubt that Marlborough showed his skill in commanding a battle very different from Blenheim. Contrary to all the rules of warfare he succeeded in getting his men across a river in face of a superior force late in the afternoon after they had had a long and tiring march. It took until late at night to round up 9,000 prisoners in the pouring rain. Philipp Muller, who worked at Nuremberg, produced a silver medal which represented Eugene and Marlborough as Castor and Pollux riding on chargers, with a Latin inscription that translates 'the stars that deliver are come'.

The reverse shows cavalry charging across the foreground while massive blocks of infantry occupy the rear, and beyond them the city of Oudenarde; clouds of smoke obscure part of the battle. Two inscriptions in Latin translate 'the slaughter of thousands of Frenchmen at Oudenarde', and 'Vendome in Flanders as in Italy runs from Eugene, proving Eugene's skill in making an enemy run'. Christian Wermuth, who worked at Gotha and Leipsig, produced a silver medal with bird's-eye views of the battlefield on the obverse and the town and fortress of Lille on the reverse. The surrender of Lille was marked by a silver medal by Boskam, with the queen on the obverse, and, on the reverse, Prince Eugene, on horseback, commanding the siege.

The siege lasted ten weeks and cost the Allies 12,000 casualties; the French had used 'throwing bombs', which appear to have contained boiling pitch. A Dutch medal commemorated the event by showing the Tower of Babel to symbolise the useless efforts of General Vendome and the Duke of Burgundy to co-operate in the defence of Lille. Details of the siege are given in the Latin inscription, and Lille is referred to by its Flemish name of Ryssel. On the reverse the fortress of Lille is under siege beneath the sun and the moon, the implication being that Louis' emblem of the sun has received a severe check. The Latin inscription is from *Joshua*, x, 12: 'Stand still, thou sun, in Gibeon, and thou moon in the valley of Ajalon'. Among other medals, one in silver by Brunner is interesting because its inscription makes clear the differing roles of Eugene and Marlborough in the siege. Eugene is described as superintending the attack while Marlborough is commanding the army which covers the besiegers. The scene shows the personification of Lille presenting the key of the city to Eugene and Marlborough, both of whom are holding lilies. The reverse has a plan of Lille. A quotation from Virgil's *Aeneid* (ii, 363) refers to it being an ancient city given back after years of domination.

This year of capitulations continued in the capture of Tournai on 30 July. Marlborough had hoped to take it earlier but a cold spring followed by heavy rains, which had washed away the roads, delayed the start of his campaign. Tournai had an elaborate system of underground galleries that made the going dangerous for the attackers. A medal struck in silver and copper, issued by

K. Lauffer, shows the siege on its reverse. The city can be seen as a background to lines of cannon, which are firing their burning shot well over the zigzagging walls. The Latin inscription records the city's surrender. On the obverse the French nation is likened to a ship in a storm, the broken mainmast denoting the loss of Lille, and the cargo, which is being thrown overboard, the surrender of Tournai. The inscription, which translates 'The huge members of the kingdom fall in ruin', comes from Virgil's *Aeneid* (ix, 708). M. Brunner also produced a medal showing Tournai besieged, with the shields of Flanders and Tournai above it; on the reverse is the figure of France seated and clasping her hands in despair, and at her feet are olive branches and masks, which refer to the unsuccessful peace proposals made by Louis to the Allies in June; in the distance a tower can be seen struck by lightning. The Latin inscriptions are taken from *Jeremiah* (iv, 10)—'Ah, Lord, they will cry, you have deceived this people utterly. You promised peace to them and here the sword cuts to the very soul'—and from *Exodus* (xx, 7)—'You shall not use the name of peace in vain'.

The battle of Malplaquet, fought between a gap in the forests of Sar and Lagnieres, was costly for Marlborough, since he lost a fifth of his men; and, though the French were forced to withdraw, the victory was really theirs, for an invasion of France had been prevented. Croker commemorated the event with a silver medal showing the battle being fought out in the forest, with Victory flying overhead, and an inscription claiming success for the Allies; the obverse has a portrait of the queen.

Another year of capitulations for medallists to commemorate was 1710, starting with the surrender of Douay on 29 June. Brunner struck a medal showing a plan of the town and its fortress on the obverse, and Pallas Athene snatching half a thunderbolt from Jupiter on the reverse. But the most interesting medal of the year was Dutch, struck in silver, which shows Anne as Delilah cutting off the hair of Louis XIV, who is seated asleep in a tent; in the distance a town is seen under bombardment. The reverse shows Louis as a decrepit, gouty old man dancing to the harp Anne is playing.

Naturally numerous medals were struck to mark the end of the War of the Spanish Succession. A cast and chased silver medal was produced in Holland to commemorate the opening of the peace conference; on its obverse are the figures of France, Spain, England, Austria and Belgium seated at a table discussing the treaty, while the reverse shows a sketchy view of Utrecht beneath the name Yahweh incorrectly spelt and above the city arms. The inscription announces that the conference began on 29 January 1712. Croker produced a gold medal showing the bust of the queen on the obverse and the queen again, as Britannia, on the reverse, holding an olive branch, spear and shield, and gazing at labourers working in the fields and merchant ships at sea, symbols of the return to peace.

THE UNION OF ENGLAND AND SCOTLAND
An event of great significance in British history was the Union of England and Scotland in 1707. The Union sprang from a real danger of war between the two countries rather than from any love between them. It offered the Scots a guarantee for their Presbyterian church and £398,085 towards solving their economic plight, while for England it ensured the Hanoverian succession. The Union set up the largest common market area in Europe, and led to forty-five Scottish MPs joining the House of Commons and sixteen elected Scottish peers the House of Lords (not until the 1963 Peerages Act were all hereditary Scottish peers allowed to sit in the Lords). The Scots accepted the terms, but the ominous sign of thirty-one dead whales washed up on the Firth of Forth made the superstitious fear their loss of nationhood. Croker struck a medal in gold and silver to mark the great occasion. The obverse has the bust of Queen Anne wearing her crown and the order of the Garter. On the reverse is the royal coat of arms, surmounted by the crown and resting on a pedestal bearing the royal monogram. On either side the lion and unicorn stand as supporters, holding the shields of England and Scotland, while below are two sceptres in a crossed position with the collar of the Garter.

Although it was hoped that the Act of Union would discourage support for the Jacobites in Scotland, the very next year the Old Pretender set out from Dunkirk for that country. His preparations had been delayed when he caught measles, but on 6 March the expedition set sail with five men of war and twenty frigates and a force of some 4,000 men. The government's secret service already knew their plans and had stationed Admiral Byng with thirty-two ships off the Firth of Forth ready to intercept them as far from Dunkirk as possible. One ship was captured and the rest turned back.

Medallic propaganda material had been prepared by Norbert Roettier, who had fled to France in 1695 to escape a charge of taking dies from the Mint. His medal shows the Old Pretender dressed in armour and cloak, with the inscription, 'Cuius Est' ('Whose is it?'). On the reverse is a map of the British Isles with its capitals marked by initial letters, and some ships in the sea; the inscription is 'Reddite igitur' ('Therefore give it back'). Clearly these medals were to be distributed to supporters.

Several medals were struck to commemorate the expedition's defeat. Hautsch issued a satirical silver medal with the queen's portrait on the obverse and a scene of the French fleet being chased by Byng, with a lengthy Latin inscription which translates 'The attempt of the French on Scotland frustrated by the vigilance of our mighty Anne'. Another inscription reads 'fugere non fallere triumphus' ('if you cannot win the trick, get away')—which is a perversion of Horace's 'fallere et effugere est triumphus' ('win the trick and get away'). Croker produced a silver medal with the bust of Anne on the obverse, and Britannia, armed with spear and shield, defending Scotland, while the French fleet can be seen retreating, on the reverse. Smeltzing's medal also had the bust of the queen on the obverse, and the rose and thistle intertwined around a sceptre surmounted by an eye, while in the distance prisoners can be seen being led to the Tower of London. The lengthy Latin inscription refers to the capture of one Jacobite ship, the *Salisbury*, with Lord Griffin and the two sons of Lord Middleton on board, and it is they who are being taken to the Tower. Martin Brunner, a colleague of Hautsch, produced a silver medal with the bust of the queen on the obverse, and the reverse showing an ass about to devour a thistle but being driven back by the smell of a rose held by a woman. The ass represents the Old Pretender, the thistle Scotland, and the woman is Anne.

JACOBITE LEANINGS

Among the lighter subjects discussed during the reign of Queen Anne was the fascinating case of Dr Henry Sacheverell, shown by

2

3

4

5

Page 113, The Later Stuarts (IX)
(1) and (2) The Pretender's restoration, 1709; (3) The Pretender's attempt,
1708; (4) Dr Sacheverell, 1710; (5) The Jacobite attempts of 1708 and 1716.

two medals. He had carefully chosen the date of 5 November (1709) to preach a sermon in support of the High Church doctrine of non-resistance and passive obedience to a king who ruled by divine right, a doctrine committing him to the support of the Stuart succession to the throne. This was a direct attack on the Act of Settlement of 1701, which had laid down that the Hanoverians should succeed, and Dr Sacheverell found himself facing impeachment, a political trial in which the House of Lords acted as both judge and jury, the House of Commons presented the prosecution case, and the prisoner was left to defend himself as best he could. The verdict was given on 20 March 1710, when the Lords found by sixty-nine to fifty-two votes that he was guilty and then proceeded to punish him mildly by forbidding him to preach for three years.

This outcome suggested that the Jacobites had a real chance of securing the throne, for the highest court in the land had supported the Hanoverian succession by only a narrow majority. Consequently, there was a split in the Tory party between supporters of the Jacobites and Hanoverian successions, for the Old Pretender now seemed a better bet. November 5 had been the day of the Gunpowder Plot's discovery and the landing of William III, and had an ominous meaning in the history of English monarchy.

Sacheverell's opponents issued several satirical medals, one of which, cast in silver, showed his bust in canonical robes on the obverse and a bishop's mitre on the reverse, with the inscription 'Is firm to thee'. If the mitre was meant to suggest that the episcopal bench of the Lords was behind Sacheverell, it was misleading, for the bishops were evenly divided in their voting on the case. A second cast silver medal shows the same obverse but the bust of Pope Innocent XI on the reverse; again the legend is 'Is firm to thee'. This pope had died in 1689, and the reason for his appearance on this medal is to be found in a resolution appended to the sentence on Sacheverell, which stated that the decree issued by Oxford University in 1683 supporting passive obedience to kings was to be publicly burnt by the common hangman. Thus the portrait of Innocent XI was a piece of subtle satire that contemporaries would easily have understood.

The Sacheverell case led to the issuing of a pro-Jacobite medal by N. Roettier, who had already struck numerous medals for the

Old Pretender and his father, James II. His 1710 silver medal has the head of the Old Pretender on the obverse, proclaiming him James III, and shows sheep in a field on the reverse, with the Latin inscription 'Cognoscunt me meae' ('they know me and mine'). As Anne neared her death in 1712 a copper-gilt medal was cast and chased by Roettier for circulation among Jacobites in England. The obverse shows James in armour and cloak, and again the inscription claims that he is James III. The reverse has the bust of Princess Louise, his sister, who died in 1712.

Chapter Five

The Hanoverians

GEORGE I

George I was proclaimed King of England on 12 August 1714, and the event was marked by the usual issuing of commemorative medals. One shows his bust on the obverse, and a map of Europe with a large 'Horse of Hanover', its hindlegs in Hanover and its forelegs in Britain, on the reverse. The outline of Europe is noticeably inaccurate. Another was issued in gold by Ehrenreich Hannibal, who was born at Stockholm in 1678 and was in service with George at the time of his accession. The obverse of his medal shows George in armour and cloak, with an inscription accrediting him with his new titles, and also the issuer's name. The reverse shows the king, wearing his Electoral cap and supported by figures representing Religion and Liberty, being presented with the crown and sceptre from Britannia, who steps over the dead body of a monster representing the lost Jacobite cause. The inscription gives the date of the proclamation in both the Julian and Gregorian calendars, 1 and 12 August.

George arrived in England on 18 September and was crowned in Westminster Abbey on 20 October. Opinions differ today as to whether Hannibal's coronation medal was the official medal or not; most favour Croker's. Hannibal's medal was struck in gold and silver and shows the bust of the king, laureated, in armour and cloak, on the obverse, with his titles and Hannibal's name. The reverse shows George, seated under a canopy and holding his sceptre, being crowned by Britannia, who is holding a shield; the inscription gives the old and new dating of the ceremony. Croker's coronation medal was struck in gold, silver and copper and is quite common. The obverse has a bust of George, laureated, in armour and cloak, with his titles for an inscription, together with Croker's initials. The reverse shows the king seated in his robes, being crowned by Britannia, who is holding a spear and shield. There is no canopy over the king as in Hannibal's medal. The inscription gives the date of the coronation.

George marked the year of his coronation by issuing a numerous range of medals to Indian chiefs in North America. One in both bronze and brass shows the bust of George in armour on the obverse with the words 'George, King of Great Britain', and an Indian drawing his bow on a deer which is standing on a hill on the reverse. Another version in copper and in brass shows an Indian throwing a spear at a deer on its reverse.

THE JACOBITES AGAIN

Croker marked the defeat of the 1715 Jacobite Rebellion by the issue of silver commemorative medals. One marked the defeat of Squire Forster's men, who surrendered at Preston on 13 November 1715. They had started their revolt by marching from the west coast across the Cheviots, intending to head southwards down the east coast, but when they recalled the strength of the Newcastle garrison, they retraced their steps to the west coast and proceeded as far south as Preston, where they frittered the time away with the local girls until trapped by General Carpenter, who received the surrender of 1,600 of them, including Forster; he is reputed to have said 'that he was not fit for the post he was in, was sorry for what he had done, and wept like a child'. Croker's medal has the bust of George in armour and cloak, with an inscription listing his titles and Croker's initials, while the reverse shows a trophy of arms on a pedestal at whose base are seated two naked captives; the inscription gives the date of their surrender.

Croker's second medal marked the battle of Sheriffmuir, with the same obverse as his first but with the figure of Victory carrying sword and palm and driving the rebel cavalry before her on the reverse. An amusing and rare satirical medal was struck in silver to mark the failures of both the 1708 and the 1715–16 Jacobite attempts at revolt; the medallist was Christian Wermuth, a native of Altenburg who worked at Gotha and Leipsig until his death in

1739. The obverse has the bust of James in armour and cloak, with the inscription 'Nihil efficiens' ('Nothing works out'). The reverse has an interestingly distorted map of the British Isles surrounded by ships and a Latin inscription parodying Julius Caesar: 'Bis venit, vidit, non vicit flensque recessit' ('Twice he came, he saw, he did not conquer, and he fled in tears').

If the Jacobites had little to celebrate with medals in 1715 and 1716, they made up for it in the following years by marking any event they could to keep alive their cause. In 1719 the Old Pretender's betrothed, the Princess Clementina Sobieski of Poland, escaped in male clothes from Innsbruck, where she had been held by the Emperor Charles VI to please the British government, which was against her marriage to the Pretender. She reached Bologna and there was married by proxy to James, who was then in Spain. Otto Hamerani, a papal medallist, struck a number of medals for the Pretender, one of which celebrated her escape. On the obverse Clementina is shown in gown and mantle, wearing jewels in her hair, with an inscription implying that she is queen of England. The reverse shows her in a carriage drawn by two horses galloping at full speed from a city, which can be seen in the distance, just as the sun is rising. Hamerani was also responsible for striking a silver medal to mark the birth of their child, Charles, the Young Pretender, on 31 December 1720. The obverse has the busts of James and Clementina, whom the inscription acknowledges as king and queen, together with Hamerani's name, while the reverse has a female figure (Providence) holding an infant in her left arm, and pointing with her right arm at a globe, turned to show the British Isles, thus drawing the child's attention to the kingdoms that are to be his. The Latin inscription describes Providence as the midwife, and gives the date of the birth.

A rare lead medal marked the exposure of the 1722 Jacobite conspiracy, which came fully into the open in May 1723. The obverse shows Bishop Atterbury, the Earl of Arran, the Earl of Orrery, Lord North and Lord Gower seated at a round table making their plans. The Latin inscription is arranged chronogrammatically: 'DeCretVM est regno brIto restItVatVr abaCtVs' ('It is decreed, let the banished one be restored to the throne of Britain', MDCCVVVVII = 1722). In the exergue is the word 'conspiratio' ('the conspiracy'). The reverse shows the same people falling backwards off their chairs as lightning descends from the Eye of Providence, which looks down from clouds above them. Again the Latin inscription is chronogrammatic: 'ConspIrate aperIt DeVs et Vos fVLMIne pVLsat' ('Conspire! God discovers and smites you with his lightning', MDCLLVVVVIII = 1723). Atterbury was deprived of his see and banished for his part in the plot, and it was some time before the Jacobites were ready to strike again.

DOMESTIC AFFAIRS

One interesting pewter medal struck in 1717 commemorates the founding of the Westminster Fire Office. On the obverse is a portcullis with a crown above it and the Prince of Wales' feathers; the inscription reads 'Westminster Fire Office established 1717'. The reverse bears an oak wreath. Gold versions were struck for the directors and silver for the clerks, so presumably the lead medals were for publicity. The only way to guarantee the appearance of a fire-engine at one's house if it caught fire was to take out an insurance policy with a firm offering a fire-fighting service. The Westminster Fire Office offered such a coverage at a rate of 60p (12s) for every £100 of insurance, and 8½p (1s 8d) for the mark (badge) that was attached to the outside of one's house for identification by the firemen. By 1780 the company had six fire-engines and thirty-six firemen, who were paid according to the fires they attended (6d for a chimney fire and 2s 6d for a more serious fire). With orange and blue uniforms, they wore iron helmets and carried hatchets and 'preventers', long hooks for pulling buildings down.

Sir Robert Walpole found he could not exercise sufficient patronage by creating new Knights of the Garter, so he resurrected the Order of the Bath. In 1725 Walpole and thirty-seven others were given the new honour, the occasion being marked by the issue of a medal in gold, silver and copper by J. Croker. The obverse depicts George I, and the reverse shows the four-year old Prince William dressed as a Knight of the Bath. The inscription translates, 'the other hope' (heir?), 'The Order of the Knights of the Bath revived and its decorations augmented, 1725'.

GEORGE II

Croker's medals for the coronation of George II and Queen Caroline on 11 October 1727 were struck in gold, silver and copper in large quantities and are common today. He struck a separate medal for each of them. The king's medal has the laureated bust of George II in armour and cloak, with an inscription giving his titles. The reverse shows George seated on the Coronation Chair, holding the sceptre and the orb, and being crowned by Britannia, who is holding a cornucopia and resting on a fasces; the Latin inscription translates 'By a willing people crowned 11 October 1727'. Croker's medal for Queen Caroline shows her wearing a coronet, while on the reverse she is standing between the figure of Religion, who is holding a book, and Britannia, who holds a spear and shield; the Latin inscription translates: 'This, my affection; this, my country; crowned 11 October 1727'.

In 1730 Croker produced the obverse of a medal of the royal family struck on the king's orders for presentation to foreign princes and others he wished to honour. It has the busts of the king in armour and the queen, with their names and the date. The reverse was made by Johann Sigmund Tanner, who was born in Saxe-Gotha and had come to work in the Mint in England. On Croker's death in 1741 he was promoted to the post of Chief Engraver, which he held until his death in 1773. The reverse has the portraits of the seven royal children with the Prince of Wales in the centre; the names of the two princes and five princesses are given in the inscription. A separate copper medal was struck for Frederick, Prince of Wales, by James Dassier, who was born in Switzerland and worked in Rome and London (where he was Assistant Engraver). The obverse shows the Prince in armour, and the reverse has the coronet, feathers and motto of the Prince of Wales, supported by two infant angels in the clouds.

Frederick's eldest son was George III, who became king on George II's death in 1760, as his father had died in 1751. Frederick quarrelled with his father, and so became the centre of political opposition at his home, Leicester House. There he worked out detailed cabinet lists ready for the day of his father's death, and a complete timetable of what he would do to secure political power when his father died, down to each minute of each day, though allowing a reasonable few hours to see to the funeral of his father a few days after his death. His own death came first, however, so we shall never know whether those elaborate plans would have come off.

WARS AND TREATIES

Medallists of George II's reign show the usual preoccupation with foreign affairs, particularly treaties and battles. The first half of the eighteenth century in European politics emerges almost like a Scottish dance, countries alternately joining hands in peaceful alliance, and splitting into two lines facing each other; then partners swop places, the line-up alters, and war looks inevitable until a circle of alliances is formed again. Sir Robert Walople built up his own circle of alliances, culminating in the Second Treaty of Vienna in 1731, which was the subject of a medal struck in gold, silver and copper by Croker. On the obverse is the head of George II, while on the reverse is Neptune in his sea-chariot contending with four winds, which he is succeeding in calming. The treaty has calmed the countries concerned—England, France, Spain, Holland and Austria—and produced what has been described as an Anglo-Austrian understanding, an Anglo-French entente and a Franco-Spanish concord. It was achieved by Walpole reversing the foreign policy of England for the previous six years and persuading George II to put England before Hanover, and as such is a demonstration of Walpole's power.

No medal commemorates the loss of Captain Jenkins' ear, which was cut off by Spanish coastguards when they waylaid his ship, the *Rebecca*, and bound him to the mast. But the outcry in Parliament following the incident showed Walpole that many merchant MPs desired a trade war. In an effort to prevent one he promised to negotiate with Spain for damages for Jenkins and the other 180 ships' crews that had been molested by guarda-costas over the years. The resulting agreement, known as the Convention of El Pardo, was signed, for Britain, on 14 January 1739 by Benjamin Keene, the British Envoy in Spain. Spain agreed to pay £95,000 for damages done by guarda-costas. Disputes over the settlement, such as the War of Jenkins' Ear, soon broke out, but before that every village in England was displaying placards with the words 'No Search', and anti-Spanish medals had been struck. One copper

Page 122, The Hanoverians (I)
(1) and (2) The Jacobite conspiracy, 1723; (3) Revival of the Order of the
Bath; 1725; (4) Convention of El Pardo, 1739; (5) Battle of Porto Bello, 1739.

medal shows Keene dressed in Spanish clothes and holding a purse, while in the distance behind him can be seen two armed men pursuing a third man towards some ships. The inscription reads 'Don Benjamin made the Convention. Braveo'. On the reverse a cloaked Spaniard is seen leaning against the base of a column, with a full purse lying at his feet. The inscription reads 'All's undone. No Search. £95,000'. Another copper medal has the figure of Britannia seated and leaning on her shield while brandishing a drawn sword and uttering the words 'I'll revenge my wrongs'. The reverse shows a British soldier with drawn sword standing over a vanquished foe, with the words 'Britons strike home'. This medal was probably made by James Roettier for Mr Pinchbeck, the toyman.

Admiral Edward Vernon (1684–1757) was to be the subject of a number of popular medals in the early stages of the war for his naval exploits, but no medal exists to mark his most lasting claim to fame—the introduction of the grog ration, which was finally ended in 1970. He introduced this mixture of a quart of water with a half-pint of spirits to improve sailors' diet, and it was christened 'grog' after his well known grogram (mixture of silk, mohair and wool) cloak. During the numerous debates in the Commons about the outrages perpetrated by the Spanish guarda-costas, he had been one of the government's strongest critics, declaring that he could take Porto Bello in the West Indies with six ships. In July 1739 he was sent out to burn the shipping there, and, having six ships, he decided to exceed those orders and capture the port, which he did in two days. He became the hero of the hour, for he had proved by his action how negligent the government had been in not tackling the Spanish threat to our trade. Among the numerous medals struck to mark the event was a brass one showing the admiral in his uniform, with a ship and Fort Chagre in the background, above which was inscribed 'A view of Fort Chagre. The British glory revivd by Admiral Vernon'. The reverse shows the English fleet in Porto Bello harbour, with the inscription 'He took Porto Bello with six ships only. Nov.22.1739'.

His attack on Carthagena on 4 March 1741 was commemorated by more popular medals, one of which was made in pewter. The obverse shows the admiral in his uniform, with Carthagena behind him, and is inscribed 'Adml Vernon viewing the town of Carthagena'.

The reverse shows the English ships outside the harbour, while within it is a boat marked 'Don Blass—He destroyed the forts of Carthagena, April 1741'. The story of what happened is not really a happy one in spite of the medals hailing Vernon's leadership. He had led a fleet of thirty ships with 10,000 soldiers on board in what was the biggest invasion fleet yet sent by any country to the West Indies. For his part he did his share in destroying the forts at the harbour entrance and so making the soldiers' landing easy, but General Wentworth, an inexperienced and obstinate man, wasted so much time preparing batteries and laying out camps that the Spaniards were able to continue their resistance while the English troops died like flies in the unhealthy climate. In April Vernon re-embarked the force, which had now been reduced to some 3,500 men.

In 1741 there was an outburst of feeling against Walpole for his failure to conduct the war vigorously enough; for years politicians had grumbled under his premiership and now they felt they could bring him down. A number of medals were struck to this end. One copper medal shows Admiral Vernon holding a sword and a staff, with a cannon in front of him and a fort behind, and the legend 'The British glory reviv'd by Admiral Vernon'. The reverse shows the devil leading Walpole by a rope round his neck towards the mouth of the infernal beast; out of the devil's mouth is a label worded 'Make room for Sir Robert', while in the exergue are the words 'No Excise'. Walpole had been roundly attacked, though not by means of a propaganda medal, for the excise duty he had proposed in 1733 and this was now being brought against him again. Clearly the medallist seeks to contrast Vernon's efforts with Walpole's lethargy. Laurence Natter, later Assistant Engraver to the Royal Mint, issued a lead medal showing the bust of Walpole, with a Latin inscription which translates 'Robert Walpole, Knight of the Order of the Garter'. The reverse has a statue of Cicero holding a scroll in each hand, with the legend (in Latin) 'He governs minds by eloquence' (Virg, *Aen*, i, 157). Walpole had been made a Knight of the Garter in 1726, a great honour for a commoner. But another version of this medal exists with the reverse inscription reading 'He governs minds by money', and yet another, whose Latin edge-engraving makes the point more strongly—

Page 125, The Hanoverians (II)
(1) Walpole and the Devil, 1741; (2) Walpole kicked out, 1742; (3) Carlisle
taken, 1745; (4) Battle of Culloden, 1746; (5) Execution of Jacobites, 1746.

'He governs minds by money, and by money is himself governed'.

In the following year Walpole was forced to resign and his resignation was medallically noted. A rare lead medal shows him seated, with his left elbow resting on a bag of money and his right hand holding a paper inscribed, 'Jan 18 1742'; the inscription reads 'I am kick'd out of doors'. The reverse shows a gateway with a head stuck on top of a pole above it, and is labelled 'No screen'. This refers to Walpole's nickname of 'the Screen', which he acquired by protecting members of parliament after the South Sea Bubble. The design on the reverse is a pun on his name (Wall-pole), and the head on the pole suggests that he is a traitor. His resignation was softened by the grant of a peerage, the earldom of Orford, and this is recorded on a copper medal of Natter's. The obverse has a bust of Walpole with the words 'The right hon. Robert Earl of Orford', and the reverse shows Britannia trampling upon Envy, and placing a coronet on Walpole's head; he is dressed in a peer's robes. The inscription reads 'Envy shall not prevail against thee. MDCCXLII'.

It is fitting that a medal should have been struck to commemorate George II's part in the battle of Dettingen in 1743, for he was the last King of England to lead his men into action. Daniel Haesling, who worked at the Hamburg Mint, struck the medal in gold and silver, producing a fine piece of work by the standards of those days, with a true representation of the distant landscape and low relief of the land in the battle scene on the reverse, where George appears in the foreground on horseback; the obverse has the bust of the king in armour and cloak. George commanded an army of 49,000 English, Hanoverian and Hessian troops, who had marched along the right bank of the River Main pursued by some 60,000 French troops on the left bank. The French moved faster and succeeded in getting ahead of George and crossing the river on pontoons to occupy the village of Dettingen on the right bank. When George arrived, his army was bombarded by the forces on the left bank, and after three hours the French in Dettingen broke their strict orders and left the security of the village to attack him across a marshy ravine. George dismounted and, sword in hand, led his troops into the advancing French infantry, routing them and forcing them back to the river, in which many of them were drowned in a vain attempt to reach the further bank. The victory forced the French to evacuate Germany.

A not uncommon brass medal by an unknown artist was struck to commemorate the naval action against the Spanish and French fleets outside Toulon harbour in February 1744. This is a fascinating medal, for each part of it is alphabetically labelled, suggesting that it must have been accompanied by an explanatory leaflet. The obverse has a body hanging from a gallows in the foreground and a naval action in the background, where one ship is in flames. The letter 'A' is above a ship, 'B' labels the body, 'C' the upright of the gallows and 'D' the cross-piece; below is the date '1743/4'. On the reverse, ships, marked 'F' and 'G', and troops are assaulting coastal fortifications, 'E', while, in the foreground, two officers, marked 'H', are talking, while nearby a lion fights a cockerel 'I'. Something of the medallist's message can be gathered from an examination of the story of the battle. The Spanish fleet had been given shelter in Toulon harbour and Vice-Admiral Thomas Mathews, who had returned to active service in 1742, was given the task of watching the harbour until both French and Spanish fleets left it. Unfortunately he was not on speaking terms with his second in command, Richard Lestock, and, when the enemy came out and the pursuit began, while Mathews and Captain Cornewall of the *Marlborough* and Captain Hawke of the *Berwick* did some good work in the van of the chase, Lestock, in command of the rear, ignored his orders, which he said he did not understand, and took no part in the fight. Then Mathews failed to follow up the enemy, who escaped with little loss. A national outcry followed and in the following year the Commons insisted on a court-martial for the two admirals, nine of the captains and four lieutenants. Mathews and five captains were cashiered, two captains were placed on half-pay, and two acquitted; another captain who was to have been tried absconded. All the lieutenants were acquitted. Lestock, properly the most guilty of all, was honourably acquitted for clinging to the letter of the law.

THE '45

The 1745 Jacobite rebellion inevitably attracted the attention of medallists and its major events were duly marked. In France a copper medal was struck by way of publicity for the faithful to mark the expected coming of the Young Pretender. On the obverse appears the head of Charles, whom the inscription labels Prince of Wales, while on the reverse Britannia, with spear and shield, is standing on the shore watching the approach of a fleet; the inscription is 'Amor et spes' ('Love and hope').

The threat of invasion led loyalists in England to form defence associations, some of which issued medal-badges. One copper medal shows two men wearing the badge of some club and grasping right hands. The inscription reads 'Where hearts are right, let hands unite. Founded in the French war 1745'. The reverse has a coat of arms showing St George piercing the shield of France; the coat of arms is supported by a lion and a two-headed eagle, with Britannia as a crest. The inscription reads 'These banners spread, are Gallia's dread'. The exergue tells us that the maker was J. Kirk, St Paul's Churchyard. Another loyal association medal was struck in copper by Thomas Pingo. The obverse has a general on horseback reviewing troops, and a Latin inscription which translates 'For our king, our altars, and our hearths'; it is dated 4 November 1745. The reverse shows Pallas overthrowing giants while Jupiter is flying by on his eagle. The Latin inscription translates'What can they avail, rushing against the clanging aegis of Pallas'.

After advancing as far south as Derby, Bonnie Prince Charlie turned and retreated to Scotland. Carlisle, which he had taken in November 1745, was surrendered to the Duke of Cumberland on 30 December, and the event was marked by several medals. The Danish engraver Johann Henrick Wolff (1727–88) made a copper medal bearing the bust of the Duke of Cumberland, with a (Latin) inscription: 'William, Duke of Cumberland, the favourite of the soldiers, born 15 April 1721'. The reverse shows the Duke dressed as a Roman warrior, his shield decorated with a portrait of the King, attacking the Hydra of Rebellion; Carlisle can be seen in the background. The inscription translates 'The rebels driven from England and Carlisle reduced, Dec. 1745'. Mr Pinchbeck, the toyman, arranged to have a copper medal struck with the Duke of Cumberland on the obverse and again on the reverse, this time on horseback, directing a soldier to conduct two rebels to the rear. The inscription reads 'Rebellion justly rewarded at Carlisle Dec.

1745'. This **medal** is poorly executed and easy to find. A badly **made common** copper medal has the bust of the duke on the obverse and **the rebel** army retreating on the reverse accompanied by the inscription 'The Pretender's last shift or rebels race for life, 1745'. Another copper medal marking the rebels' retreat has a portrait of George II on the obverse, and a map of the British Isles, guarded by ships and by a hand from heaven holding a flaming sword, on the reverse. A translation of the Latin inscription on the reverse reads 'He accomplishes marvellous things, 1745' (based on Psalm 98, verse 1).

The famous battle of Culloden, fought on 16 April 1746, saw the end of Charlie's hopes, for his 5,000 half-starved and exhausted men were soundly beaten by Cumberland's fit 9,000. Numerous medals were struck to mark the event. Wolff's medal appeared in silver and brass, bearing the portrait of Cumberland on the obverse and the battle scene on the reverse. The Duke is on horseback in the foreground, while immediately behind him is the River Spey, which he had forded with his army; in the distance one arm of the cavalry can be seen rushing through a walled enclosure, while another arm is pursuing the fleeing rebels. The Latin inscription translates 'In a moment civil discord has been suppressed at Culloden, 16 April 1746'. John Kirk produced a silver medal with the Duke on the obverse and a different battle scene on the reverse. Again the Duke is on horseback, but this time he is riding over a prostrate foe who has the heads of the King of France, the Pope and a Scot; broken swords, chains, etc. lie on the ground and in the distance is a view of the battle: 'By courage and generalship he defeated the Scottish rebels at the morass of Culloden, 16 April 1746', states the inscription (in Latin). Mr Pinchbeck issued poor-quality brass medals with the Duke on horseback on the obverse and battle scenes on the reverse. On one of them the battle scene consists of the rebels fleeing before two files of infantry and a cavalry charge; a cannon and a dead horse are in the foreground. Another shows the Duke commanding the battle, in addition to a similar battle scene. In both cases the inscription reads 'Rebellion justly rewarded at Culloden 16 April 1746'.

The Gentleman's Magazine for 1746 contained these lines in connection with Mr Pinchbeck's medals.

To me 'tis quite plain, tho' some folks seem amaz'd,
Why the duke should by Pinchbecke on medals be rais'd;
For who is more proper, all wonder to smother,
Than one man of metal to strike up another?

A poorly executed copper medal faced the reality of the aftermath of Culloden on its reverse by showing an executioner hanging a rebel while two others are begging for mercy from another executioner, who is holding the robe ready for them. The inscription reads: 'More rebels a comeing'. The obverse has the Duke of Cumberland galloping along on horseback with a drawn sword. A proposal that Cumberland should be made a member of one of the City Companies was commented on by a Jacobite, who said that the Butchers' Company would be the most suitable. James Wolfe, future hero of Quebec, refused to shoot a wounded prisoner when the Duke ordered him to do so. Apart from ordering the slaughter of rebels, Cumberland ordered girls to ride naked on horseback for the amusement of his troops. But the best-selling medal that year was not one showing a scene from the battle. It was one executed by Richard Yeo (d 1779), who became Assistant Engraver to the Mint in 1749 and Chief Engraver in 1775. On its obverse it had the bust of the Duke and on the reverse the Duke, as Hercules, trampling on Discord and raising up Britannia, with a Latin inscription recording the defeat of the rebels at Culloden. It was produced in a range of metals, the silver selling at a guinea each, the copper at half a guinea and the gold for two guineas, all selling at more than the value of their metal.

In 1747 Admiral Anson defeated the French fleet under de la Jonquière when it left harbour with convoys for Canada and the East Indies; and Thomas Pingo, who was to become Assistant Engraver at the Mint in 1771, struck a gold medal to mark the event. On the obverse is the head of Anson being crowned by Victory, who is standing on the prow, 'George Lord Anson, Vict. May III. MDCCXLVII'. The reverse shows Victory with a wreath and trophy standing on a sea-monster, which is above a glove, with the inscription 'Circumnavigation; Saunders, Brett, Dennis, Campbell, Keppel, Saumarez. MDCCXL. MDCCXLIV'. The reverse refers to Anson's famous circumnavigation, 1740–44, in which he was sent to attack the enemy in the Pacific and found that the only return route was round the globe. His squadron has been described as the worst equipped ever to have been sent on such an expedition. Instead of soldiers, he had Chelsea pensioners, all of whom died on the voyage. None of his marines had ever fired a musket; none of his six ships had a chronometer and the flagship was nearly wrecked due to bad miscalculations. But his capture of the *Acapulco* with treasure which would be valued at some £3 million today, was a magnificent prize. By the time he reached China he had only one ship left, the *Centurion*, with 201 men, the first British warship the Chinese had seen. Scurvy hit the crew, and an unknown pamphleteer, posing as the ship's chaplain, wrote an interesting account of the disease in *A Voyage Round the World by George Anson*, explaining that the disease would cause old wounds to open up.

Anson's real distinction lies in his later work in naval administration, for he improved the design of ships and introduced a proper system of classifying them, made blockading tactics more effective, started a permanent Marine Corps, introduced uniforms to the navy and began a system of retirement pensions. To him must go the honour of forging the navy into a weapon capable of winning the all-important Seven Years' War, 1756–63.

The War of the Austrian Succession was brought to an end by the Treaty of Aix-la-Chapelle in 1748, and this was marked by a Dutch silver medal showing a priestess performing a sacrifice at an altar, beneath a female figure holding a cornucopia, an olive branch and a pair of scales; there is also the lion of Holland resting on a Bible and holding a staff with a cap of liberty. The reverse has the eight shields of the countries signing the treaty—England, France, Austria, Spain, Holland, Sardinia, Italy and Prussia—and in its centre is a burning heart pierced with arrows. The Treaty was saluted in England by a massive firework display on 27 April 1749 in London's Green Park, for which Handel composed his *Royal Fireworks* music. The display took five months to prepare and was to include a royal brilliant wheel, 'whose fire is thirty feet in diameter and is moved by twelve fires'. The display began hours late due to quarrels between the Italian fireworks experts and the crowd. Handel's music had finished before the fireworks began, and the event, costing £14,500, was brought to an end by a thunderstorm at midnight.

The Treaty did not mean the end of the Jacobite cause, as Prince Charles was quick to remind the English, by issuing a copper medal showing a Highlander with drawn sword and shield, and a Latin inscription which translates 'Who can contend with me? I will leave no stone unmoved to obtain that. 1749'. The reverse has a rose and an inscription translating 'My affairs are at issue'. This probably refers to the clause in the treaty by which the King of France recognised George II as king, which in turn led to Prince Charles having to leave France.

An extremely rare silver medal records Charles's secret visit to London in September 1750, during which he was received into the Church of England at St Mary-le-Strand church; his abandonment of Roman Catholicism suggests that he was considering a rebellion in England rather than in Scotland. The medal has a collection of arms round a shield bearing the cross of St Andrew, and an abbreviated Latin inscription which translates 'The secret conference assembled for consultation was presented with this medal by order of James in 1750'. The reverse has a thistle, with the Latin inscription 'May it flourish and prick'.

The last serious Jacobite attempt on the British throne was the Elibank Plot of 1752, encouraged by the death in the previous year of the Prince of Wales, leaving as George's heir the thirteen-year-old George (III). The plot called for the assassination of the royal family and the immediate seizure of London, but it had to be abandoned when the Prussians failed to supply help and one of Charles's agents was captured. The silver medal marking the attempt was probably executed by Thomas Pingo. On its obverse is a portrait of Charles with the (Latin) inscription 'May he, the great genius of Britain, return'. The reverse shows Britannia standing by a rock on the seashore, and resting upon her spear and shield, waiting for the arrival of an approaching fleet; behind her is a globe with the map of Britain visible on it. The Latin inscription reads 'Oh, long hoped-for ship. Let us rejoice, citizens, 23 Sept. 1752'.

SOCIETIES AND ELECTIONS

Among the less politically-charged medals of the first half of the eighteenth century was a gilt one, now rare, marking the formation of the Beggars' Benison Club in 1739, at Anstruther in Fifeshire. The club was ostensibly to collect 'good' songs, stories and jokes, but in reality to offer its members an outlet for exuberant and outrageous fun. Its members were drawn from all classes, including noblemen and some members of the royal family. The entrance fee was 10 guineas, and, on joining, the new member paid 3 guineas for a highly illuminated diploma and a gold badge valued at 5 guineas. The medal shows on its obverse the naked figures of Adam and Eve holding hands, while a lion lies at their feet; the inscription reads 'Be fruitfull and multiply'. The reverse shows Venus recumbent beneath a canopy with Cupid at her side, while Adonis, spear in hand, stands with a dog by a tree; the inscription reads 'Lose no opportunity'.

In 1750 the Free British Fishery Society marked its foundation under the governorship of Frederick, Prince of Wales, by having a medal struck in gold, silver and copper. The Society's aim was to encourage the establishment of fisheries in the North Sea. Its medal was designed by Ludwig Koch, a German engraver who worked at Gotha from 1750 to 1793. On the obverse is the bust of the Prince of Wales, in armour and mantle, with the inscription 'Frederick Prince of Wales Governor of the Society'. The reverse has a fishing boat hauling in its nets, while in the forefront men can be seen on the shore moving barrels, and the inscription 'For the advantage of Great Britain, Free Brit. Fishery by a society establ. 1750'.

Reverting to politics, election medals were to be a feature of the late eighteenth and early nineteenth centuries but were rare in the middle of the eighteenth century. An interesting example is a silver medal struck for the Louth election of 1 November 1755. Its obverse has the figure of Hibernia standing on a rock in the middle of the sea and assailed by four winds blowing from the mouths of four faces; the inscription is 'Firm to our country as the rock in the sea'. On the reverse is a heart and two united hands; its inscription is 'By our strict union in Louth we disappointed the hopes of our enemies on the 1 of Novem 1755 in the 29 year of the reign of K. Geo. the II whom God long preserve. May the lovers of liberty never lose it'. The story behind this medal is that a number of people formed an Independent Club to resist the influence of the propertied clique and succeeded in ousting a Mr Bellingham and electing Thomas Tipping.

On the same day as the citizens of Louth won their election battle an earthquake destroyed Lisbon, killing some 30,000 people. This event shattered the complacency of many Englishmen who had abandoned their religion. London had suffered two slight earthquakes in 1750 and 'earthquake gowns' had been invented. John Wesley wrote a book entitled *Serious Thoughts on the Earthquake at Lisbon* in which he examined the geological causes of the London and Lisbon earthquakes before concluding that God must have shaken the earth. Parliament voted £100,000 for the Lisbon victims, and much of the sum was used to send grain and rice there. A very rare Dutch silver medal by Matin Holtzhey shows English, Dutch and Spanish ships hurrying to Lisbon on its reverse. The obverse shows a female representing Lisbon seated amid broken columns while lightning and flames spring from a cleft in the ground near her feet.

An unusual silver medal or badge was cast and chased when the Eddystone lighthouse was rebuilt in 1757. Its obverse shows two sailing ships near the lighthouse; its Latin inscription translates 'For the safety of all, Eddystone rises again, 1757'. The reverse is plain. The first lighthouse was completed in 1700 but destroyed by a fierce storm on 26 November 1703. A second was built in 1709 and destroyed by fire on 2 December 1755. The first stone of the third was laid on 12 June 1757 and it was finished on 18 September 1759. To prevent the seamen involved in the rebuilding from being press-ganged into the navy, each of them was issued with this medal-badge, which is pierced for suspension.

THE SEVEN YEARS' WAR

The second half of the 1750s was to see the beginning of the crucial war between England and France, the Seven Years' War (1756–63), which naturally was the subject of numerous medals.

A scarce brass medal by an unknown artist struck in 1756 has an interesting story behind it, for it is concerned with Admiral

Byng's failure to save Minorca from French attack. The obverse has the half-length figure of General Blakeney, the garrison commander at Minorca; on one side of him three cannons are firing, while on the other side is a ship. The inscription reads 'Brave Blakney reward. But to B give a cord', the 'B' referring to Byng. The reverse shows a three-quarter-length figure of Byng receiving a purse from an outstretched hand, and behind him is a ship. The inscription poses the question 'Was Minorca sold by B for French gold?' When the siege of Minorca began, it was learnt that no less than thirty-four officers, including the four colonels of the regiments stationed there, were absent from their place of duty; but the gallant old General Blakeney held on for seventy days until 28 June.

Although Byng was a long-serving admiral, he had never commanded an action before, and he was known for his lack of initiative; yet in spite of this the Duke of Newcastle, the Prime Minister, sent him with ten ships, half of which were leaky, under-manned and under-gunned, to try and relieve the garrison. Byng took a month to reach Gibraltar and there learnt that the siege had been going on for a fortnight, but he still waited six days before seeking out the French fleet. When the encounter took place, it was indecisive, but Byng withdrew, leaving the garrison to its fate. This disaster led Newcastle to fear a popular outcry, led by Pitt, so he decided to place the blame firmly on Byng's shoulders; and when he heard the enemy's reports of what had happened, he proceeded to blacken Byng's name without waiting for Byng's own report, which he eventually had published in a distorted form. A show was made of arresting Byng and he was tried by court martial on a charge of negligence; the court reluctantly sentenced him to death, the only penalty, but suggested mercy. However, Byng was shot on his own quarter-deck on 14 March 1757.

The Minorca incident was an early episode in the Seven Years' War. The war was fought in North America, India and Europe, so its medals are best considered in three sections, rather than chronologically. Though a substantial number of forts were captured from the French in North America, surprisingly few captures are marked by the striking of medals. Thomas Pingo struck a silver medal to mark the capture of Fort Louisburg on Cape Breton

Page 136, The Hanoverians (III)
(1) and (2) Loss of Minorca, 1756; (3) Battle of Plassey, 1757; (4) American Indian, 1757; (5) Louisburg taken, 1758.

Island: its obverse shows a globe, inscribed 'Canada America', which rests on a prostrate fury at the edge of a rock, who drops fleur-de-lis and points to some boats at sea; on either side of the globe are a grenadier and a Canadian, while above is the figure of Fame, an English flag and a scroll inscribed, 'Pariter in bella'. The reverse shows Louisburg under siege, showing the fort and ships, with the inscription 'Louisburg taken MDCCLVIII'. The edge is engraved with the names of Boscawen, Amherst and Pitt. Louisburg was a vital port for the French as it was the nearest ice-free harbour to the St Lawrence River, which freezes from November to May. If William Pitt, now war minister, was to capture Quebec by sending an expedition up that river he had first to ensure that Louisburg was taken. Admiral Boscawen was in charge of the naval side of the expedition. Brigadier James Wolfe had already decided that to sail into the harbour would invite bombardment from the harbour guns and had worked out a plan to land some way from Louisburg and attack it from the rear, when Major-General Amherst arrived from England to take command. Pitt had just promoted Amherst from the rank of colonel, so that he had moved from below to above Wolfe's rank, and in order to assert his new authority he scrapped Wolfe's plan and ordered a frontal attack. The French held their fire until the English were close in and then let fly so that Amherst was lucky to capture his objective.

In the following year Wolfe, now a general, led the expedition up the St Lawrence to Quebec, with Admiral Saunders in command of his fleet. The famous climb up the cliff to the Heights of Abraham was the bright idea of Wolfe's three brigadiers when his own efforts had failed. Luck was on Wolfe's side when he attacked on 13 September, for on that night the French sentries were expecting a convoy of their own boats to pass by, not knowing of its cancellation; also the captain at the point called Anse de Foulon, where Wolfe landed his troops, had allowed most of his men to go home for a few days to get the harvest in, while a whole French battalion had been withdrawn from the Heights of Abraham, unknown to General Montcalm as they were not under his command. The Society for the Promotion of Arts and Commerce, which issued a number of medals in connection with this war, had a silver medal struck with the head of Britannia above a laurel-wreath uniting a trident and a standard. Wolfe's and Saunders' names are inscribed on it. On the reverse is the figure of Victory, a captive seated and bound and the prow of a ship; the inscription reads 'Quebec taken. MDCCLIX', and at the bottom 'Soc. P.A.C.' General Wolfe figures on a silver medal struck by C. Gosset and J. Kirk, the obverse of which shows him in armour and cloak, while the reverse has an urn on a pedestal inscribed 'Pro Patria', under a laurel wreath with arms and flags. The date of his capture of Quebec is given in the inscription.

The capture of Montreal and the completion of the war in Canada was marked by another of the SPAC's medals. Struck in silver, it shows the head of George II on the obverse, and a weeping female figure seated beneath a pine tree near a beaver on the reverse; the inscription reads 'Canada subdued. MDCCLX. S.P.A.C.'.

In India the struggle against the French and the Nawab of Bengal was marked by the atrocity of the Black Hole of Calcutta, which Robert Clive set out to revenge at the battle of Plassey, 23 June 1757. Clive's total force numbered some 3,000, the majority of them native mercenaries, sepoys. His artillery consisted of eight 6 pounders and two small howitzers. Facing him were 35,000 infantry, 15,000 cavalry and 53 guns (32- and 24-pounders). These heavy guns each needed forty oxen to pull them and an elephant to push. Defeat for Clive would have been inevitable had not the young Nawab's uncle, Mir Jaffir, decided to desert his nephew in order to gain the throne for himself. He kept a considerable number of the Nawab's forces out of the battle and Clive's losses were only eighteen killed and forty-five wounded. The SPAC issued a silver medal to record the victory. On the obverse the figure of Victory, with a trophy and a palm, is riding on an elephant; the inscription reads 'Victory at Plassy Clive commander. MDCCLVIII Soc. P.A.C.' (Note the inaccuracy of the date; the battle was fought in 1757.) On the reverse Clive is seen dressed as a Roman warrior, holding a standard in his left hand and presenting the Nawab's sceptre to Mir Jaffir; between them are a globe, cornucopiae and a rudder. The inscription reads 'Injuries attoned, privilege augmented, territory acquired. A soubah given to Bengal. MDCCLVIII'.

Clive's portrait, three-quarter-length, and wearing an embroidered coat, ribbon and star, is to be found on a copper medal struck in his honour in 1766, when he was Governor and Commander-in-Chief in Bengal. The inscription reads 'Robert Clive Baron of Plassey' (the title of his Irish peerage). The reverse shows the figure of Fame pointing to an obelisk listing Clive's achievements; it is inscribed 'Honour the reward of merit. Anno 1766'. Who struck the medal is obscure, for on the obverse are the initials 'I.V.N.', which may stand for John van Nost, while the reverse has 'C.G.' which indicates C. Gosset, who struck the medal of General Wolfe mentioned above.

In Europe the British task in this war was to support her ally Frederick of Prussia, who was attacked on all sides by France, Austria and Russia. On 1 August 1759 an English and Hanoverian army, numbering some 42,000, beat the French army of Marshal Contades, which numbered 54,000, at Minden. The event was marked by a silver medal struck by Johann Georg Holtzhey, a native of Amsterdam who worked for Frederick of Prussia, and occasionally for Louis XV and Louis XVI. The obverse of his medal shows Mars armed with scourge and shield, surrounded by French arms and flags, dispersing the enemy, who are to be seen flying the field in the distance; the Latin inscription translates 'Numbers give way to virtue', adding the name and date of the battle. The reverse has a view of the valley of the River Weser; in the foreground is an olive tree entwined with a vine, and in the base keys in a mural of crowns and wheatsheaves. The brunt of the battle was borne by six English infantry regiments, which carry the name 'Minden' on their colours today.

The Treaty of Paris of February 1763 ended the Seven Years' War for England and the event was marked by the issuing of a silver medal by J. G. Holtzhey. He shows Mars and Austria as two military figures conducting the helmeted Prussia to the Temple of Janus, surmounted by the arms of Russia and ornamented with various shields; within the temple, Neptune and Sol (sun) are performing a sacrifice. On the reverse a Latin inscription gives details of the various treaties signed by the different powers at the end of the war.

GEORGE III

George III began his long reign in 1760 and was married and crowned in the following year. Jakob Abraham, Engraver to the Prussian Mint, struck a gold medal to honour George's marriage to Sophia Charlotte, daughter of the Duke of Mecklenburg Strelitz. The obverse shows them dressed as Greeks, with an inscription giving their names and titles. The reverse has Britannia burning incense at a tripod, and holding a staff with a cap of liberty; in the distance is a ship. The Latin inscription states that Britannia is making her offerings. The medal is dated 10 September 1761, though the marriage had in fact taken place two days earlier.

Johann Lorenz Natter, who had worked in Florence before he came to London, under the patronage of the Duke of Devonshire and the Duke of Marlborough, to take up the post of Assistant Engraver at the Mint, was responsible for issuing two official medals for the coronation, which took place on 22 September 1761. The obverse of the first has the bust of the king, in armour and laurel-crowned, and the reverse shows him seated in Roman dress, being crowned by Britannia, with the legend 'Patriae Ovanti' ('Rejoicing in the fatherland'). This inscription is interesting, because George III was the first of the Hanoverian kings to have been born in England, a fact he emphasised when he succeeded to the throne. Natter's second medal has the bust of Charlotte on the obverse, and on the reverse shows an angel crowning her as she stands in coronation robes, holding a sceptre. The inscription is 'quaesitum meritis' ('selected by merit'). Both these medals have the date of the coronation on the reverse. John Kirk, who worked for the Society of Arts and had his workshop in St Paul's Churchyard, also issued a coronation medal in silver. The obverse has the bust of the king in armour and cloak, and the reverse that of the queen, with an inscription giving the dates of their marriage and coronation.

The early years of George's reign saw the issue of a number of interesting medals, such as two struck to mark the connection of the Rev William Stukeley with Stonehenge. He developed the idea that druids were connected with the building of Stonehenge (though modern research has shown that it was there 800 years before the druids). The first medal appeared in 1765 with the portrait of Stukeley in high relief on the obverse and a view of

Stonehenge on the reverse. The second was struck in 1796 by Thomas Wyon, senior, showing Stonehenge surmounted by a druid's head, and on the reverse a complicated mathematical diagram of druidic calculations.

One can only speculate about the reason for the making of one medal to be found in the British Museum and the Salisbury Museum. On the obverse it is roughly engraved by I. Levi with a map of the road junction at the top of Harnham Hill just south of Salisbury; also shown are a pit, a church, a gallows and a building marked 'CH' (court house?), with the inscription 'J Curtis alias Curtel hung in chains Sarum Mar 14, 1768'. The reverse is inscribed 'Dec 28, 1767, for the robbery and murder of Wolf Myers'. The body of Myers, a Jewish pedlar, was found in a pit near Coombe, partially covered by snow. A large knife lay near him and the inquest showed he had died from a fractured skull and a stab in the stomach. Curtis, a sailor, who had passed through Salisbury the same day as Myers, was arrested on board his ship, the *Achilles*, at Gosport. In his possession was a pedlar's box and a printed handbill similar to one found on the body. Curtis denied to the last that he had committed the murder, even when shown the site before he was hung.

Sir John Fielding, the blind magistrate of Bow Street, was at the height of his successful battle against crime when J. Kirk commemorated his efforts in 1774 with an oval medal; it has his bust with open-necked shirt, flowing hair and staring eyes on the obverse, and a Latin inscription on the reverse which translates 'The blind old man examines the violent and punishes them'. With his brother, Henry Fielding, John had established the Bow Street Runners, a band of detectives whom one could hire for a guinea a day plus 70p (14s) expenses; started the *Hue and Cry*, which is now the *Police Gazette;* and introduced a night patrol system for London of sixty-eight men divided up into thirteen groups under a 'conductor', who was paid 25p (5s) a night, and armed with two pistols, a carbine and a cutlass.

The voyages of exploration of Captain Cook were marked with medals; a gold one struck by Barnett for his second voyage in 1772 has the head of George III on the obverse and two ships on the reverse with the words 'Resolution, Adventure sailed from England,

Page 142, The Hanoverians (IV)
(1) The Curtis murder, 1767; (2) John Wilkes, 1774; (3) Captain Cook, 1772; (4) Sir John Fielding, 1774; (5) Lord George Gordon, 1780; (6) John Wesley, 1789.

March MDCCLXXII'. Cook's ship was the *Resolution*. He returned from this voyage having lost only one man from scurvy, a triumph due to his insistence on cleanliness and the drinking of limejuice. His third voyage in 1776 was marked by a medal in gold, silver and copper issued by the Royal Society, which depicts him on the obverse with a Latin inscription which translates 'James Cook, the most ardent explorer of the Ocean'. The reverse shows Fortune holding a rudder and standing beside a globe; its Latin inscription reads 'Our associates leave nothing untried'. His death in 1779 was marked by a medal in white metal with his bust on the obverse, and the inscription 'Kill'd by the Indians at O'why'hee, February 14, 1779' on the reverse.

Even the religious work of John Wesley and George Whitefield was marked by the issue of medals. John travelled 224,000 miles in fifty-three years preaching his Methodist gospel, dipping his pen into the inkwell attached to his saddle in order not to lose a moment's chance of writing. In old age he used a coach fitted out as a study. A medal struck in copper and white metal in 1789 has a portrait of him on the obverse, and pictures him on the reverse preaching beneath a tree to a large audience: 'By grace are ye saved through faith, Anno domini 1789'. Another marked his death in 1791, with a portrait on the obverse and the rays of the sun enclosing the inscription 'Well done, good and faithful servant, enter thou into the joy of thy Lord' on the reverse. George Whitefield, who started his education at the Gloucester cathedral school (King's School), turned Calvinist in the end, preaching sermons that gripped his audiences. He was the subject of a number of copper medals, one of which has his portrait on the obverse and the inscription 'An Israelite indeed. A true soldier of Jesus Christ. Died 30 Sep. 1770 in y 56 year of his age' on the reverse. Another, again with his portrait on the obverse, records 'the funeral sermon preach'd by the Rev John Wesley, AM, from Numb C 23 v10 "Let me die the death of the righteous and let my last end be like His".' The Countess of Huntingdon financed some of Whitfield's work and one of the churches she built can be seen in Brighton. Thomas Wyon, senior, struck a medal in both copper and white metal in her honour; it has a picture of her wearing a bonnet on the obverse, 'Selina, Couns dowr of Huntingdon', and the inscription

'I know that my redeemer liveth. Ob 17 June 1791 aet 84' on the reverse.

The political aspect of organised religion is shown by a silver medal marking the failure to secure the abolition of the Test and Corporation Acts in 1790; these Acts prevented Dissenters from holding any public office. On the obverse is the king standing beside a church tower and a monument inscribed 'Bill of Rights and Magna Carta'; below is the inscription 'May our happy constitution in church & state ever continue unimpaired. Church and King Club, Manchester'. The reverse reads: 'The third attempt of the dissenters in the short period of three years to obtain a repeal of the Corporation and Test Acts, those barriers of the British Constitution, was frustrated in the House of Commons by a majority of CLXXXIX March 11 MDCCXC'. Not since Anne's reign had there been such an outcry in defence of the national church.

Philanthropists were not forgotten by the medallists and in 1790 W. Mainwaring struck a medal to commemorate the death of John Howard, the prison reformer. On the obverse is a portrait of Howard and on the reverse a Latin inscription praising his services to mankind and giving his age as sixty-five. A lesser-known reformer, Captain Coram, who established the Foundling Hospital for abandoned children, was commemorated in the year of his death by J. Porter's gilt and bronze medal. The obverse shows a swarthy-looking man, with the inscription 'In memory of the foundling's friend, 1805'. The reverse is inscribed 'Foundling Hospital instituted 17 October 1739, Thomas Coram Founder'. A basket was always left outside the hospital to receive abandoned babies; both Hogarth and Handel gave generously to its establishment.

Edward Jenner of Berkeley in Gloucestershire, who discovered that injections of cowpox could prevent people catching smallpox, was commemorated in 1796 by a medal struck in Berlin. The obverse has the bust of Jenner and the reverse shows a cow garlanded by a flying angel, while children hold hands and dance round it.

THE AMERICAN WAR OF INDEPENDENCE

Among the commemorative medals of George III's reign are some remembering the American War of Independence. Only one cause of the war seems to have been marked: in 1766 the Stamp Act, which had extended stamp duties to America, and thereby met bitter opposition, was withdrawn and this was the subject of two medals. One has the head of the Prime Minister, Rockingham, on the obverse with the words 'The restorer of commerce, 1766. No Stamps'. Its reverse has a ship and 'Thanks to the friends of liberty and trade'. The second has William Pitt the Elder's head on the obverse, and the inscription 'The man who having saved the parent pleaded with success for her children' on the reverse. This medal was struck by T. Pingo and the inscription refers to Pitt's winning the Seven Years' War against France and then his concern for the colonies.

The first military victory to be marked by a medal was the American recapture of Boston in 1776. B. du Vivier of Paris struck a copper medal with the head of George Washington on the obverse and a Latin inscription describing him as the supreme leader, and on the reverse a battle scene showing four officers on horseback in the foreground together with cannons and barrels, the wall of a fort and troops lined up on the shore watching ships crossing the bay. Benjamin Franklin, who sought the aid of France for his fellow Americans, was the subject of an anonymous medal in 1777, which shows him wearing a cap on the obverse, while the reverse shows a tree struck by lightning; the Latin inscription translates 'The lightning does not respect useless things, 1777'. Franklin was known for his experiment of sending a kite up during a thunderstorm. In the same year the English General Burgoyne surrendered his army after the battle of Saratoga, when General Howe failed to arrive to assist him. Burgoyne had marched his men south from the St Lawrence Valley to the River Hudson under difficult conditions, hampered by the green wood from which 500 carts had been made, from lack of horses, too many soldiers' wives and a shortage of food (1,000 men were lost hunting for food). The medal was struck by N. Gatteaux and has the bust of General Gates on the obverse, and on the reverse a picture of Burgoyne surrendering his sword to Gates in front of the English troops, who are laying down their arms, and the Americans, who stand with colours flying. The Latin inscription translates 'Enemy surrendered at Saratoga on 17 Oct 1777'.

Page 146, The Hanoverians (V)
(1) Recapture of Boston, 1776; (2) John Paul Jones, 1779; (3) Virginia, 1780; (4) Siege of Gibraltar, 1783; (5) Slave, 1787.

In 1779 the war was brought home to Scotland when Captain John Paul Jones in the *Bon Homme Richard* captured the frigate *Serapis* and threatened Edinburgh. Augustine Dupré issued a copper medal with the bust of Jones on the obverse and a naval battle scene, with bodies in the sea, on the reverse; the Latin inscription records the capture. The same year saw the acquittal of Admiral Keppel after trial by court-martial for failing in his duty as commander of the home fleet. He was the unfortunate victim of political intrigue; his acquittal gave the opposition in Parliament an opportunity to denounce the government and part of this anti-government campaign was the issue of a number of medals. One struck in silver-gilt has the bust of the admiral on the obverse and the inscription 'Judicious, brave and gallant', on the reverse. The other has a similar obverse, and a female holding sword and scales standing over a terrified figure on the reverse, with the words 'Justice triumphant and malice defeated, Feb 11 1779'.

An anonymous Virginian propaganda medal appeared in 1780, the obverse showing a clay pipe and a female warrior, sword and spear in hand, standing on top of a fallen man whose crown has rolled off; the inscription on the obverse reads 'Rebellion to tyrants is obedience to God'. The fallen figure is George III. On the reverse a white man and an Indian are seated by a tree looking at ships passing, with an inscription 'Happy while united, 1780'. On 3 November 1780 the Continental Congress ordered silver elliptical medals to be struck to mark the capture of Major Andre of the British army behind American lines on his return from West Point, where he had secretly arranged with the commanding officer, Benedict Arnold, for the betrayal of the garrison in order to let the British up the Hudson. Unable to return as planned, Andre had changed into civilian clothes and been guided to within a short distance of no-man's land, before accidently falling into the hands of Americans wearing English greatcoats. They found the terms of the agreement in the sole of his boot and the plot was foiled. Because Andre was not in uniform he was hung as a spy in spite of British protests; a monument was erected to him in Westminster Abbey. The medal has a heart-shaped shield with the word 'Fidelity' on a scroll on the obverse, and the reverse has a wreath of fleur-de-lis, and a Latin inscription translating 'Love of country conquers'.

A whole range of medals was struck to commemorate the Spanish siege (1779–83) of Gibraltar, which held out under General Elliot. A silver one shows the siege in progress on the obverse and Elliot on the reverse. L. Pingo produced one with an 'aerial' map of the bay and the Rock with ships going into an attack which the inscriptions says was made on 13 September 1782. The reverse has a lengthy inscription in praise of the defence of Gibraltar.

The Treaty of Versailles, which ended the American War of Independence, was marked by a number of medals, one of which has an Indian greeting Britannia, with the date 4 September 1783 on the obverse, and a diagram of circles on the reverse enclosing the names of the States; 'American Congress, we are one' is in the centre.

POLITICAL PROPAGANDA

Political propaganda medals in the reign of George III include a large number celebrating the career of John Wilkes and his fight for freedom. He edited the *North Briton*, and in its forty-fifth edition denounced the government for incompetence, which landed him and his entire staff in court. The judge rejected the arrest warrant as it was made by a government minister, and in so doing upheld the argument that subjects have the right to criticise their government. Wilkes was hailed as the champion of the free press and 'No 45' was chalked up everywhere. Wilkes went on to become the champion of free elections to Parliament by battling on to win the 1768 election for Middlesex. Though he won, Parliament refused to accept him until six years later. One 1768 medal has 'Wilkes & Liberty, 45' on the obverse, and 'Poll'd for Middlesex 1292' on the reverse. Another has the bust of Wilkes on the obverse and 'May true Britons enjoy liberty and property without oppression' on the reverse. His return to Parliament in 1774 was marked by a medal, struck in several metals, which depicts him wearing the Lord Mayor's chain of office on the obverse; on the reverse a head appears out of a boot, together with an axe and the inscription 'Britons strike home'. The reverse is probably a punning reference to the Earl of Bute, who was Prime Minister in 1762.

In 1780 Wilkes helped the king to put down the Gordon Riots, named after Lord George Gordon. This week of anti-Catholic protests in fact showed the discontent of the period rather than specifically anti-Catholic feeling. Lords and MPs had to defend themselves with drawn swords, and the Bishop of Lincoln had to escape over the rooftops dressed in female clothes. When the distilleries were broken into, Lincoln's Inn water supply became alcholic! Gordon was acquitted on a charge of treason, since the prosecution failed to prove his link with the rioters. An anonymous medal marked the event with a portrait of Gordon on the obverse, and the inscription 'L Geo Gordon tried and honourably acquitted by a virtuous jury Febry 5 1781' on the reverse.

Medals were struck in 1788 and 1789 to mark the king's recovery from a bout of porphyria (then believed to be insanity). One medal struck in various metals has the head of the king on the obverse, and the Garter badge on the reverse, with the words 'Cheltenham, 1788'; while another has a female with a snake, together with the bust of the king on a pillar, on the obverse, and the archway leading to the spa on the reverse. The inscription shows that it was issued by S. Moreau. Although Fox and the Prince of Wales employed Dr Warren to ensure that the king remained too ill to rule, Pitt's Dr Willis succeeded in nursing him back to health by playing chess with him and the flute to him, though occasionally strapping him in what was known as the *coronation chair*. Willis issued a medal with his own head on the obverse and the inscription 'Britons rejoice your king's restored, 1789' on the reverse. George's thanksgiving visit to St Paul's is recorded on a medal issued in silver and copper by L. Pingo. The obverse has a portrait of the king, and the reverse shows the sun shining over the city of London arms and is inscribed 'Visited St Paul's 23 April 1789'. Criticism of the Prince of Wales's attitude towards his father is refuted by a gilt medal with the prince's bust on the obverse, and a crown with the words 'He holds for the king, 1789' on the reverse.

The year 1789 witnessed a growing struggle for power between Charles Fox and William Pitt. William Lutwyche (Birmingham) struck an election medal for Fox which has his portrait on the obverse with the words 'Glory be thine intrepid Fox firm as old Albion's batter'd rocks', and on the reverse

Page 150, The Hanoverians (VI)
(1) George III's recovery, 1789; (2) Dr. Willis, 1789; (3) William Pitt the Younger, 1789; (4) and (5) Charles James Fox, 1789.

Resistless speaker, faithful guide,
The courtiers' dread, the patriots' pride.

A white-metal medal depicts Fox on the obverse, and 'The free and independent electors of Westminster, 1789' on the reverse. The inscription is probably a reference back to the 1784 Westminster election, when the king ordered 280 guardsmen to vote for Fox's opponent, and the Duchess of Devonshire distributed kisses to Foxites; Pitt had pressed Parliament to look into that election in a vain effort to unseat Fox. In 1789 a white-metal medal showed a portrait of Pitt on the obverse, and on the reverse 'The supporter of the Constitution of old England'.

Threats to the constitution were made by many who were sympathetic to the ideals of the French Revolution, and their activities are recorded on medals. Tom Paine, whose writings inspired many, was the subject of one medal. On the obverse is a church and a tree with a body hanging from it; from the mouth of the victim come the words 'I die for this my damn'd book'. He is holding the book in his hand and above is written, 'Tommy's *Rights of Man*', and round the rim, 'A tree is known by its fruits'. The reverse is inscribed: 'May the tree of liberty exist to bear Tommy's last friend'. Another medal shows him hanging beside the words 'End of pain'. His 6d book called for universal suffrage, the sovereignty of the people, new marriage and divorce laws, family allowances and maternity benefits, free education, prison reform, full employment, a graduated income tax and international arbitration.

Treason charges failed to stick when applied to Paine's supporters T. Hardy, Horne Tooke, and J. Thelwall, and they celebrated their acquittal with a medal struck in bronze and white metal. The obverse has their portraits, while the reverse has the portraits of their counsel, V. Gibbs and T. Erskine, surrounded by the names of the jurors (including the author's relative, Matthew Whiting). Thomas Hardy had a separate medal in white metal struck: the Tower of London and a wharf surmounted by the scales of justice held by a hand from heaven appear on the obverse, with the inscription 'Thos Hardy acquitted Nov 5 1794'; the reverse lists the names of his jurors. Horne Tooke had one with his portrait on the obverse and the Old Bailey on the reverse. The London

Page 152, The Hanoverians (VII)
(1) Tom Paine hanging, 1793; (2) Trial of Tooke, Hardy and Thelwall, 1794; (3) Trial of Hardy, 1794; (4) Three Loggerheads, 1797; (5) Attempt on George III's life, 1800; (6) Charles James Fox, 1806.

Corresponding Society celebrated the acquittal of Daniel Eaton
with a medal showing a cock and 'Struck by order of the London
Corresponding Society' on the obverse; a list of jurymen and
'The King versus Eaton, 14 March 1794' appear on the reverse.
The trade tokens connected with the Society and these trials should
be compared with the medals (see my *Trade Tokens*, pp 123-7).

The London Corresponding Society was the subject of some
fascinating medals in 1797, when three of its agents were tried for
subversive activities, including a meeting held at Warwick on 31
May. A bronze and white-metal medal shows a donkey cart
containing three persons (Binns, Thelwall and Jones in all prob-
ability) stopped beneath a beam with three nooses; to the left is a
crowd labelled 'Wrongheads' and to the right another labelled
'Rightheads'. The inscription reads: 'Greatheads meeting at
Warwick May 31, 1797'. The reverse is inscribed 'As if from Temple
Bar some head was cut and on rebelling trunk the face was put'.
Another medal shows three people hanging over a donkey cart,
with the words 'The end of three Loggerheads'. The reverse reads:
'As if from Newgate cells, three felons led and on the New droptyd,
till dead, dead, dead'. Bertie Greathead had called the meeting
to put forward his political views. Binns was tried in August for
advocating the use of force to reform Parliament; during his eleven
and a half hour trial, Dr Samuel Parr, an ardent supporter, sat in
front of the jury and glared at them while the prosecution presented
its case and smiled when the defence spoke, with the result that
Binns was acquitted. Distantly descended from Catherine Parr,
Samuel was a noted scholar whose wig had once been filled with
gunpowder by his pupils!

THE FRENCH WAR

In 1797 England came near disaster in her struggle against the
French. William Mossop struck a copper medal to celebrate the
fortunate abandonment of the French expedition to capture
Ireland. The obverse has a wreath within which is inscribed
'Friendly Association. Bantry Garrison', while the reverse shows
ships in a storm with a Latin inscription attributing the dispersal
of the invasion fleet to God; it is dated January 1797. The story
behind this medal is interesting. On 19 December 1796 an enemy

fleet had set sail from Brest to take Wolfe Tone and 15,000 troops to capture Ireland. Although they were only intercepted by one English ship, confusion arose due to the deterioration of the weather and to the fact that the ships were overcrowded with soldiers and undermanned with able seamen. Tone wrote: 'We have made 300 tacks and not gained 100 yards in a straight line'. On Christmas Day the temperature dropped to 0°F, the storm reached its height and the fleet returned to France.

The French expedition to Bantry Bay was only part of the enemies' invasion plans for 1797, for the Spaniards and the Dutch sent their fleets in due course and medals were struck to mark their defeats. J. G. Hancock issued a copper medal recording the defeat of the Spanish fleet off Cape St Vincent on 14 February 1797. On the obverse is the bust of Sir John Jervis, the admiral in command of the English fleet; he was made Earl St Vincent as a result of the victory. His birth date is given as 26 January 1735 on the inscription, and Hancock inscribed his own name on the admiral's sleeve. The reverse shows the figure of Spain seated weeping on a rock, leaning on a shield, while in the distance is the naval battle; an inscription gives the number of ships engaged and captured, and the date of the battle. Jervis had sighted the enemy fleet at five in the morning and realised that they greatly outnumbered him. The enemy had the giant four-decker *Santissima Trinidad* in its fleet of thirty-nine ships. Jervis had fifteen battleships of which only two carried 100 guns each. As one gunner on the *Goliath* put it 'We gave them their Valentines in style'; the enemy withdrew at nightfall leaving Jervis the winner.

Two copper medals were struck by Hancock to commemorate the victory over the Dutch at Camperdown on 11 October—one for the commander, Admiral Duncan, who became Viscount Duncan of Camperdown, and the other for his second-in-command, Sir Richard Onslow. The first has the bust of Duncan in uniform; it is inscribed with his name and new title, and the words 'Admiral of the White born July 1, 1731', with 'Hancock' inscribed on his arm. The reverse shows a sailor nailing an English flag to a masthead; the inscription gives the date of the battle and details of the number of ships engaged, ending with 'Heroic courage protects the British flag'. The second medal, which is scarce today, has a three-quarter-length portrait of 'Sir Richard Onslow, Bart. Admiral of the Blue. Born 23 June 1741', with 'Hancock' on his arm. The reverse shows the battle at its height, and is inscribed 'Second in command Octo.11.1797; in the *Monarch* of 74 guns broke the rear of the Dutch line & took the Admiral's ship'. The *Monarch* was Onslow's ship, in which he captured the *Jupiter*, the Dutch vice-admiral's flagship. The two fleets were evenly matched, having sixteen battleships each, though the Dutch had superior fire-power; the fight was so fierce that at one time Duncan and his pilot were the only men unwounded on the quarter-deck of his ship. After three hours the enemy surrendered. Subscriptions for the relatives of the dead reached £5,000 in one day in London, and Lloyd's (the coffee house turned shipping centre) gave £52,609 for the relief of the casualties.

Of the various medals struck to commemorate Nelson's victory of Aboukir Bay, or the Battle of the Nile, the most interesting was that struck by C. H. Kuchler, a native of Flanders, who was employed by Matthew Boulton at his Soho Mint, Birmingham; it was presented to all who took part by an Alexander Davison. Admirals, commanders and captains received gold medals, lieutenants and warrant officers silver, petty officers bronze-gilt, and seamen and marines bronze. The obverse has a portrait of Nelson held by Britannia, who is standing on a rock near the sea; in her right hand she holds a laurel branch, while at her side is an anchor. The inscription reads 'Rear Admiral Lord Nelson of the Nile'. On the reverse the English and French fleets can be seen drawn up in a semi-circle in Aboukir Bay; its inscription reads 'Almighty God has blessed His Majesty's arms. Victory of the Nile. August 1. 1798. M.B. Soho. C.H.Kuchler Fec.'. Round the edge are the words 'From Alexr. Davison Esqr. St. James's Square. A tribute of regard'. The year also witnessed the extraordinary rumours that the French would invade Britain by crossing the Channel on rafts measuring 2,000 ft by 1,500 ft, powered by windmills. These rafts were expected to carry 100 cannons and two infantry divisions with artillery and cavalry! The *Gentleman's Magazine* pointed out that each raft would need 216,000 trees and would weigh 44,000 tons. The rumours resulted in pictures of the rafts being drawn and a medal being struck. The obverse shows a cluster of flags and a drum, with the words 'Britain triumphant', while the reverse shows a raft with a castle in the centre and four windmills at the corners. It is inscribed 'French folly in building rafts. AD 1798'.

If the rafts presented no threat, the people of England prepared for an invasion which they did expect, forming volunteer corps to defend their localities. These corps were the subject of a number of medals, and also trade tokens. In 1797 a medal inscribed 'Norwich Loyal Military Association, 1797' showed a soldier with musket standing at attention; the reverse had a three-towered castle and a lion. In the following year the Birmingham Volunteers issued one showing long lines of cavalry drawn up left of centre facing similar lines of infantry on the right to witness the colours'-presentation ceremony, which is being performed in the centre. Its inscription reads 'Colours presented to the Birmingham Association, 4 June 1798'. On the reverse is a long line of gallows and the words 'End of Bonepart and the French Army'. Another patriotic medal has a yeoman standing beside his horse on the obverse, and on the reverse the inscription 'Old England 2 March 1798 entd Jas Loyal. I promise to pay to the Hon Geo Yeoman or bearer the sum of TWO PENCE ON THE PERFECT ESTABLISHMENT OF PEACE & UNANIMITY FOR KING, LORDS AND COMMONS. John Bull'.

Invasion did not come and in 1799 Napoleon's presence in Egypt was marked by a medal of Thomas Wyon's which showed Napoleon on the obverse ('Napilone Buonparte General of the French Army in Egypt'), and a collection of tents, cannon and cannon balls, with the inscription 'landed at Alexandria July 12 1798. MDCCXCIX', on the reverse. It must have been issued near the time when Napoleon deserted his men to return to France.

DOMESTIC DISCONTENTS

That all was not well in England can be seen from an anonymous medal struck in copper and white metal showing a head with a wide open mouth out of which a globe is protruding, showing the British Isles; the inscription reads 'Take not what was made for all. The uncharitable monopolizer will starve the poor. More warehouse room wheat is but 22 shillings a bushel. 1800. In distress'. The reverse has an eye inscribed 'well done', and a hand with a coronet

Page 157, The Hanoverians (VIII)
(1) and (2) Birmingham Volunteer Corps, 1798; (3) Norwich Loyal Military Association, 1797; (4) French invasion rafts, 1798; (5) French invasion preparations, 1804.

wrist dropping coins into another hand, while a hat below catches some of the coins; the inscription reads 'The Charitable hand. Come all ye distressed'.

On 15 May 1800 two attempts were made to assassinate George III. The first occurred in the morning when the king attended a field-day in Hyde Park; a man standing near him was wounded by a shot. That night when the king entered the royal box at Drury Lane Theatre, a discharged soldier, James Hadfield, fired at him from the second row of the pit. A gentleman standing next to Hadfield seized him, and after a struggle he was pushed into the orchestra pit and the pistol wrenched from him. He was handed over to the Bow Street Runners, after being interrogated by the Duke of York. Meanwhile Richard Brinsley Sheridan, the playwright, hastily wrote an additional verse for the National Anthem for the audience to sing:

> From every latent foe,
> From the assassin's blow,
>   Thy succour bring;
> O'er him Thine arm extend,
> From every ill defend,
> Our Father, King, and Friend;
>   God save the King!

After an eight-hour trial in June, Hadfield was found not guilty but insane and was committed to Bedlam. There he stayed for some forty years, writing poetry on the death of his birds and cats. C. H. Kuchler struck a silver medal to mark Hadfield's attempt on the king's life. On the obverse appears a bust of the king in armour and cloak; on the reverse is an eye above an altar, with a Latin inscription telling of the people's rejoicing that their king has escaped uninjured. The date of the attempt is also given on the reverse. P. Kempson issued a medal in bronze and gilt of a similar kind.

If Kuchler's medal expressed the patriotic feeling of his day, Hancock's medal in honour of Charles James Fox, issued in 1800, suggested criticism of George's government. The obverse has the bust of Fox, inscribed with his name and date of birth, while on the reverse, inside a wreath of olive and oak branches, is inscribed 'With learning eloquence and zeal he maintains the rights of a free and loyal people. 1800'. The activities of the London Corresponding

Society and the United Englishmen, among other politically active groups, had led the government to pass the Combination Acts of 1799 and 1800, banning such organisations of intellectuals and workers because of a deep-seated fear of revolution. Fox, a leading MP, believed that no revolutionary movement existed in England to justify these acts. With such statements as: 'I know that liberty is the greatest blessing that mankind can enjoy, and peace the next', he was championing the liberal cause before 'liberal' was a political term.

The first day of 1801 was marked by the implementation of the Act of Union with Ireland, which had been passed in the previous August. The event was marked by a silver medal struck by Kuchler, which has the bust of the king in armour and cloak on the obverse, and Britannia and Hibernia, with their shields, grasping hands, on the reverse. By the Act 100 Irish MPs took their seats in the House of Commons, and 28 Irish peers and four Irish bishops joined the House of Lords. To secure Ireland's acceptance of the Act, Pitt had used patronage to the full, buying out the Protestant patrons of eighty-four borough seats at £15,000 each, so presenting a bill for £1,260,000.

THE PEACE OF AMIENS

In 1801 came the news that the army Napoleon had abandoned in Egypt had been defeated at Alexandria by Sir Ralph Abercrombie on 21 March. British troops, numbering 15,000, went ashore, fifty-eight flat-bottomed boats conveying them the last five shallow miles, but they had no horses for the cavalry, no wagons, no maps and no interpreters. The 28th Foot (the Gloucesters) and the 42nd Highlanders were surrounded and had to fight back to back, so earning the right to wear a badge on the back of their hats as well as on the front. Abercrombie died a week later from a wound. These events were marked by the issuing of a copper medal bearing the bust of Abercrombie, dressed in uniform and holding a quizzing glass to his right eye on the obverse, and on the reverse Britannia reclining at the foot of a monument inscribed 'Wounded Mar. 21. Died Mar. 28. 1801'; to one side is a palm tree, and in the distance can be seen the battle and two pyramids. The inscription is completed with 'French defeated Mar. 21 1801'.

The Peace of Amiens in 1802 proved a very temporary affair, but it was marked by the issuing of several medals, struck by J. G. Hancock. The first, in silver-gilt, has the king holding a trident and a shield, while being crowned by Victory, who is holding a palm. The reverse has a view of St Paul's Cathedral, with a Latin motto attributing the glory to God, and the date 1 June 1802, on which a public thanksgiving was held. The second medal was issued on the instructions of D. Eccleston of Lancaster in honour of England's enemy, Napoleon. The obverse has Napoleon's bust in Roman dress, with 'Inscribed to Napoleon Bonaparte by D Eccleston Lancaster'. The reverse has a map showing Africa in the west to Australia in the east, and an inscription reading 'He gave to France liberty, to the world peace. MDCCCII'. Daniel Eccleston's portrait appears on a trade token he issued in 1794 (Dalton and Hamer, Lancashire 57). He collected medals and coins, and died in 1816 in his seventy-first year. A week afterwards a notice appeared in the *Lancaster Gazette* saying he was not defunct, and including a letter Daniel had 'written' from the other world. This letter corrected errors in the newspaper's obituary notice of the writer's death, which had appeared a week earlier. It included the sentence: 'We are totally precluded from giving you poor mortals any description of this Happy Country'. The letter was headed, 'The New Jerusalem, the City of the Saints', and it was signed in this way:

> Daniel Belteshazzar
> Fitz-William
> Caracticus
> Cadwallador
> Llewellyn
> Ap-Tudor
> Plantagenet
> ECCLESTON.

In the following year, 1803, Hancock struck some copper medals in honour of members of the Addington government, which had negotiated the Peace of Amiens. One has Henry Addington's bust on the obverse, in court dress, with the inscription 'Henry Addington, Chancellor of the Exchequer & First Lord of the Treasury'. The reverse has a female figure holding a scroll inscribed 'State of the Nation', and kneeling before a pedestal surmounted by the figures

of Britannia, Justice and Time; in the distance is Westminster
Abbey. The inscription reads 'Who can withold applause.
MDCCCIII'. Nicknamed the 'Doctor' after his father, Addington
had never held political office before he became Prime Minister
in 1801; he believed victory was impossible, representing England's
war-weariness. A clear-headed man of commonsense, he had been
chosen to form a government simply because he was not a party
politician. Another of Hancock's copper medals honoured Robert
Banks Jenkinson, Earl of Liverpool, a member of Addington's
cabinet. The medal displays the bust of the earl and his name,
title and office on the obverse. The reverse shows a female seated
figure dispatching Mercury on a message; at her side is a shield,
and in the distance a ship, with the inscription 'Integrity aids
dispatch. MDCCCIII'.

In 1804 Napoleon prepared for that long-awaited invasion of
England by drawing up his army at Boulogne, and medals were
struck to mark the event. One copper medal by J. P. Droz has
the bust of the Emperor on the obverse, and Hercules tackling the
British lion on the reverse, with a French inscription saying 2,000
ships have been constructed. Another, by Jeuffroy and Jaley,
shows a plan of the invasion army drawn up in crescent formation,
with an inscription indexing the sections by number. Its reverse
displays a picture of Napoleon seated on a platform distributing
the Legion of Honour to soldiers; the inscription dates it according
to the revolutionary calendar, 'XXVIII Therm. an XII Aout
MDCCCIV'. (Thermidor was a late summer month, including
part of August.) A third medal by Jeuffroy has Napoleon's bust
on the obverse and Hercules overturning a monster (England)
with an inscription in French which translates 'Invasion of England;
struck in London in 1804'. Presumably Napoleon wished the
conquered English to believe that they had been struck in London
on his arrival there!

The best of the medals commemorating the battle of Trafalgar,
21 October 1805, was one designed by C. H. Kuchler and issued
by Matthew Boulton to all those who took part in the battle;
later it was issued in silver, bronze-gilt, bronze and white metal.
The trial strikings in copper lack the engraving round the edge.
The obverse has the bust of Nelson in naval uniform, but hatless,

with the star of the Order of the Bath; the reverse shows a view of the battle at its height, with the inscription 'England expects every man will do his duty. Trafalgar Octr. 21. 1805'. Round the edge is engraved: 'To the heroes of Trafalgar from M Boulton'.

PITT, FOX AND WILBERFORCE

1806 was marked by the deaths of both William Pitt the Younger and Charles James Fox, rivals throughout their political lives. Thomas Wyon, junior, struck a copper medal with Pitt's portrait on the obverse, and an inscription on the reverse recalling the dates of his birth and death and his public services. Wyon was appointed Chief Engraver to the Mint at the early age of twenty-three, though he was to die two years later. The importance of the Wyon family is explained below in connection with the striking of the 1812 Spanish campaign medals. Another medal struck on Pitt's death, by Webb, shows a portrait of Pitt on the obverse, and a tower rising from the midst of a stormy sea on the reverse, with the inscription 'Patriae columen decus' ('Glory and pillar of the nation').

Peter Wyon, another member of the Wyon family, struck a silver medal in honour of Fox, portraying him on the obverse, with the inscription 'Charles Jas. Fox. This illustrious patriot departed this life September 13. AD 1806. Aett. 57'. The reverse has an inscription in his praise beginning 'Intrepid champion of freedom'.

William Wilberforce's famous fight against slavery was marked in 1807 by the issuing of a medal by Webb—on the passing of the bill abolishing the slave trade. The obverse has the head of Wilberforce with long hair tied back, and is inscribed 'William Wilberforce M.P. The friend of Africa'. The reverse shows Britannia seated and attended by Justice holding a caduceus, Equity with scales, and Courage with spear and shield; overhead hovers the winged figure of Victory, holding a cross and a wreath. This side is inscribed 'I have heard their cry. Slave trade abolished. MDCCCVII'.

G. F. Pidgeon's medal commemorates the event by showing a white man shaking hands with a negro before a background of beehive huts, palm trees and negroes tilling the land and dancing round a tree; it is inscribed 'We are all brethren. Slave trade abolished by Great Britain 1807'. The reverse has an inscription in Hebrew. Earlier, in 1787, medals in gilt, copper and white metal had been issued in the fight to abolish slavery. They show a kneeling slave with chains and the inscription 'Am I not a man and a brother?' The reverse reads 'Whatsoever ye would that men should do to you, do ye even so to them'. Some of them had the negro painted black with bright red lips.

Wilberforce had been asked to take up the anti-slavery cause by the Quakers leading the movement because only members of the Church of England were allowed to sit in the Commons. Wilberforce's tireless campaign, his speeches—supported by models of slave ships showing the appalling overcrowding, and by thumbscrews, leg irons and handcuffs which he had bought in Liverpool shops—had eventually been successful.

THE PENINSULAR WAR

In 1809 there was hard fighting in the Spanish Peninsular campaign, and it was marked by the beginning of a series of National Medals, issued under the direction of James Mudie, 'to commemorate the succession of victories achieved by British arms over Napoleon'. A number of English and foreign artists were employed to carry out this series. The first, in copper, was designed by two men, Mills and Couriguer, to mark the death of Sir John Moore. On the obverse is a portrait of the general, with the inscription 'Lieut. General Sir J. Moore K.B.'; on the reverse soldiers are defending a wounded comrade against the attack of an eagle (Napoleon) with a thunderbolt, and in the background appears the prow of a ship. It is inscribed 'Death of Sir John Moore. Corunna 16 January 1809'.

Sir John was both realist and idealist, and was responsible for the development of the Light Brigade for commando-type work, aiming to abolish mechanical drill and battle lines, and to develop a unit of fighting men who could think for themselves. He encouraged team work between officers and men; merit badges were introduced, physical fitness was encouraged and punishments that robbed a man of his dignity were discouraged. All his men were taught to cook and do their own tailoring. Moore replaced their 42in Brown Bess muskets with the new 30in Baker rifle, with its seven-groove barrel; it fired only once a minute but was accurate at 300–500 yd.

The scene on the reverse of the medal refers to his death when his army was forced to retreat to Corunna through the Spanish winter with only snow for drink. He organised a superb evacuation from the harbour, but in the fierce rearguard action with the French forces he died of his wounds.

Later in the same year the Duke of Wellington won the battle of Talavera (27 July), the first of his great victories in the Spanish peninsula. Mudie's copper medal, by Mills and Lafitte, has the bust of Wellington in uniform on the obverse; and, on the reverse, the figure of Victory giving a wreath to a lion while withholding a second wreath from an eagle, and inscribed, 'Battle of Talavera 1809'. This battle won Sir Arthur Wellesley his title of Duke of Wellington.

MATTHEW BOULTON AND OTHERS

The distinguished engineer Matthew Boulton died in 1809, and his passing was marked by the striking of an anonymous medal, now rare. The obverse bears a portrait of Boulton, bareheaded, with pigtail and cravat, while below him two small angels are holding an engraving of his Soho Mint. The reverse has a lengthy inscription:

> By the skilful exertion of a mind turned to philosophy & mechanics, the application of a taste correct & refined, & an ardent spirit of enterprise, he improved, embellished, & extended the arts & manufactures of his country; leaving his establishment of Soho a noble monument of his genius, industry, & success. The character his talents had raised, his virtues adorned & exalted. Active to discover merit, & prompt to relieve distress, his encouragement was liberal, his benevolence unwearied, honoured & admired home & abroad, he closed a life eminently useful, the 17th August 1809, aged 81, esteemed, loved & lamented.

His partnership with Watt made steam engines famous, while his production of coins for several countries at his Soho Mint, Birmingham, earned him a place of distinction with numismatists. He supplied the steam press he invented to the London Mint.

Industrialisation did not always bring benefits for all, and in 1810 a white-metal medal was struck by T. Wyon, senior, to mark the resistance of Joseph Hanson, a manufacturer, to the government's refusal to agree to a minimum wage for weavers. He was charged with uttering 'malicious and inflammatory words' at a weavers' gathering, and sentenced to prison on 12 May 1809. The reverse records this fact and that 396,000 people had subscribed to buy him a silver cup. The obverse bears the outline of a loom carrying the words 'Spinning, weaving, printing'.

In the same year a medal was struck in bronze and brass to mark the imprisonment of Sir Francis Burdett, MP, in the Tower, the last political prisoner so confined. On the obverse is a portrait of Sir Francis, and on the reverse the inscription 'The intrepid Champion of Freedom, the Enlightened Advocate of the Rights & Liberties of the People'. Following in the steps of John Wilkes at the Westminster constituency, he had become a popular radical idol earlier in the century when he exposed the treatment of the London Corresponding Society prisoners held without trial at Coldbath Fields. 'Burdett and No Bastille' had then been the cry. In 1810 he objected to the Commons arresting J. Gale Jones for organising a political meeting, since Jones's action was outside their jurisdiction. The Commons ordered Sir Francis's arrest, so he barricaded himself in his Piccadilly house. Lord Cochrane sent him a barrel of gunpowder in a hackney-coach as ammunition. Police and troops were called, as a riot was feared, and in the process of taking Burdett to the Tower shots were fired and several people died. After his release he returned to parliament and finally died in 1844.

The assassination of the Prime Minister, Spencer Perceval, in 1812 was marked by two medals. W. Taylor struck the first in both copper and white metal. On the obverse is a portrait of the Prime Minister and on the reverse a tomb over which a weeping Britannia is standing; the name 'Bellingham' is inscribed at her feet, together with the words 'He lived beloved and lamented fell. Assassinated May 11, 1812'. John Bellingham was the assassin, and the second medal depicts him on the obverse with the words, 'John Bellingham executed May 18 1812 aged 42 years'. The reverse is inscribed 'Thou shalt do no murder. Assassinated the Right Honourable Spen Percival May 11 1812'. It is noticeable that the execution followed only a week after the deed. (The extraordinary story of clairvoyance connected with the murder is described in my *Trade Tokens*, p 147.)

One interesting medal of the fighting in 1812 between Great Britain and the USA was struck by Moritz Furst, a Hungarian, who became Engraver at the Philadelphia Mint in 1808. On the obverse is the bust of Captain James Jones in naval uniform, and on the reverse a picture of the engagement between his American sloop *Wasp* and the British ship *Frolic*, under the command of Captain Whingates; the Latin inscription records what happened. The *Frolic* surrendered after a ten-minute cannonade from the *Wasp*. Though the *Wasp* and her prize had to surrender a few hours later to the British ship *Poictiers*, the Americans had gained a marked, if temporary, success. Furst's medal was struck in gold for Captain Jones, and in silver for his officers.

WELLINGTON AGAIN

Wellington's campaigns in the Spanish peninsula in 1810, 1811 and 1812 were marked by the issue of a number of medals. Mudie arranged the issue of a copper medal by Petit and Dubois to mark Wellington's defence of the Lines of Torres Vedras during the winter of 1810 and 1811. The obverse shows the general in military uniform, seated in his tent and studying a map. The reverse shows the River Tagus and an orange tree and tents; the inscription reads 'Lines of Torres Vedras—the English army on the Tagus. 1810–1811'. Reticent and punctilious, Wellington was a man of no enthusiasms or illusions, and on one occasion said: 'Now I made my campaigns of ropes. If anything went wrong, I tied a knot and went on'.

He had prepared the defence lines at Torres Vedras to serve either as a holding point to enable him to evacuate his troops from Portugal, or as a launching point for a renewed campaign; it was one of his 'knots'. The map in his tent recalls the fact that he had had Portugal surveyed and mapped, on a scale of four miles to the inch, because of the poor quality of Portuguese maps. While his men held the Lines during the winter, the French besiegers faced starvation, having to eat 5,000 of their horses; as the two entrenched sides fraternised, the French would offer brandy for English biscuits.

Thomas Wyon, junior, issued a copper medal at this time in honour of Wellington's leadership, on which he pictured Wellington's head, with the inscription 'Lieut. Gen. Lord Viscount Wellington K.B. MDCCCX'. The reverse has the figure of Victory on a mountain, holding a wreath and palm; at her side is a shield with the arms of St George and Portugal impaled on it, and at her feet is a broken French standard.

Mudie's medal series for 1812 began with one struck in copper in honour of Sir Thomas Picton and the battle of Badajoz, which was won on 6 April. The obverse has a three-quarter-length bust of Picton in uniform, wearing the star of the Order of the Bath, while the reverse shows him planting the English flag on a battlement; the inscription reads 'Badajoz. Aprl. VI. MDCCCXII'. Badajoz was the key fortress of western Spain, and, if Wellington could capture it, he would be able to take the initiative for the remainder of the year. He decided to attempt an assault through a breach in the wall, a disastrous attack as it cost 5,000 lives. The attempt seemed to have failed completely when suddenly an officer galloped up to the dejected general and told him that Picton had captured the town by a diversionary attack that had involved climbing the walls with 20 ft ladders. Picton had pressed his men forward, though ladder after ladder had been dislodged and the rungs were slippery from blood. One in five died in the successful assault.

Another of Mudie's copper medals, this one struck by Mills and Gayrard, appeared in honour of Viscount Hill, who destroyed the French fortifications covering a bridge of boats over the River Tagus at Almaraz, the only line of communication between the French armies of Soult and Marmont. The action took place on 19 May 1812. The obverse has a portrait of Hill, while the reverse shows the broken bridge over the River Tagus beneath the figures of Victory and Britannia; the inscription reads, 'Almaraz. May XIX. MDCCCXII'.

Before considering the Salamanca medal by Thomas and Peter Wyon, something must be said about this remarkable family, for they dominated part of the eighteenth and most of the nineteenth centuries with their skill as medallic artists. The family originated in Cologne, where George Wyon, senior, was born. He came to England as George I's Chief Goldsmith, while his son, George, junior, served his apprenticeship under George II's goldsmith, Hemmings, before becoming a medallist at the Soho Mint, Birmingham, in 1775. George, junior, made a silver cup which the City of London presented to the famous John Wilkes in 1772.

Thomas, senior, and Peter Wyon were his eldest sons, and they worked together as die-engravers in Birmingham until 1800. In that year Thomas went to London to work in the department of the Engraver of His Majesty's Seals, of which he became head in 1816, finally dying in 1830. His son, Thomas junior, was appointed Chief Engraver at the Royal Mint in 1815 at the age of twenty-three, and in that capacity was responsible for the Waterloo medal and the great recoinage of 1816. Unfortunately he died in 1817 at the early age of twenty-five. His brother Benjamin became the Chief Engraver of Seals in 1831, and produced the Crimea Medal before his death in 1858. His son, Joseph Shepherd Wyon, took over from him, and when he died in 1873 was in turn succeeded by his younger brother, Alfred Benjamin Wyon.

Reverting to the other line of the family, Peter Wyon, brother of Thomas, senior, stayed on at Birmingham and in due course handed over to his son William. Born in 1795, he went to London in 1815 to become the most distinguished member of this distinguished family. He started as Assistant Engraver at the Royal Mint and took over as Chief Engraver in 1828. Ten years later he had the honour of being the first medallist to be appointed a Royal Academician. He produced a large number of military, academic and private medals. When he died in 1851 he was succeeded by his son Leonard, who produced medals for the wars of the second half of the nineteenth century among others.

The copper medal which Thomas, senior, and Peter Wyon struck for the battle of Salamanca and the triumphal entry into Madrid has the head of Wellington on the obverse, and a column inscribed with the names of his victories and ornamented with the shields of England, Portugal and Spain, with French arms and a standard at its base, on the reverse. The inscription on the reverse reads. 'Enter'd Madrid August XII'. Another copper medal was issued by Brenet showing soldiers advancing towards a line of mountains up which cavalry and equipment are struggling while being attacked by the figure of Victory, who is hurling thunderbolts at them; the inscription is 'July XXII. MDCCCXII. Salamanca'. The reverse has a picture of Wellington on horseback receiving a garland from some Spaniards, with the inscription 'The British army enters Madrid. Aug. XII. MDCCCXII'. This is a medal in Mudie's series.

Page 169, The Hanoverians (IX)
(1) and (2) Battle of Trafalgar, 1805; (3) Napoleon off to Elba, 1814;
(4) Battle of Salamanca, 1812; (5) Napoleon surrenders to the Captain of
the *Bellerophon*, 1815.

After weeks of manoeuvring Wellington succeeded in defeating the French army under Marmont in a forty-minute battle at Salamanca, inflicting 14,000 casualties for 5,000 received. This left the road open to Madrid, which he took on 12 August. As the triumphant procession entered the city they were given food and drinks by the pretty girls there, who strew shawls, veils and rose petals on the cobbles. But when the troops saw the appalling poverty of the people of Madrid, they set up soup kitchens for their relief.

Napoleon's exile in Elba was marked by a medal struck in copper and brass. On the obverse Napoleon is riding a donkey back to front, while the devil is pulling him along by a rope round his neck. It is inscribed 'Inseparable friends. To Elba'. The reverse reads 'We conquour to set free. Emp. of Russia, K. of Prussia, Marquis Wellington, Prince Schwartzenberg. March 31, 1814'.

The Peace of Paris, signed on 30 May 1814, inspired the issuing of a large number of medals. A silver one in Mudie's series was executed by Jean Pierre Droz, who had come to England in 1790 and worked for Matthew Boulton, then returned to Paris about 1807 to become Director of the Mint, a post he resigned in 1814. On the obverse is the head of Britannia wearing a crested helmet ornamented with a lion and olive-wreath. The reverse has Hercules, wearing a lion's skin, trampling on a French standard; the inscription reads 'The repose of Hercules MDCCCXIIII'. Another medal has the four laureated heads of the Prince Regent of England, Alexander I of Russia, Francis II of Austria and Frederick William III of Prussia, with the legend 'Nunquam videbimus eis similes iterum' ('No one will see their like again'). The reverse has the figure of a female holding a cornucopia and an olive branch, with the inscription 'Auspicium melioris aevi. Pax per Europam MDCCXIV May.XXX' ('Experience is better than youth. Peace in Europe').

The great event of 1815 was the battle of Waterloo, yet the finest medal marking it was not struck in 1815 but ordered by the Prince Regent in 1819 and in fact never issued in the end. The Prince was keen to have a really outstanding medal to issue to the allied sovereigns and the two commanders, Wellington and Blucher. Benedetto Pistrucci was employed for the task. He was born in Rome in 1784, and began his study of gem- and cameo-cutting so young that his works were being sold as antiques when he was only sixteen years old. In 1815 he came to England; two years later he was appointed Chief Engraver at the Mint, and in 1828 Chief Medallist. From 1819 to 1849 he worked spasmodically on the dies of the Waterloo medal, but by then only Wellington of those for whom the Prince Regent had intended the medal was alive, so the dies were never hardened and no medals struck. Only impressions made by electrotyping exist. The obverse has the busts of the Prince Regent, Francis II of Austria, Alexander I of Russia and Frederick William III of Prussia side by side. Flanking them are the seated figures of Hercules and Justice, while above is the personification of the sun, riding in a chariot drawn by four horses preceded by Castor and Pollux (they had been responsible for saving the Romans at the battle of Lake Regillus in 476 BC), and followed by Zephyrus and Iris; below is the figure of Night riding in a two-horse chariot called a *biga* attended by Furies and Fates. The reverse has Wellington and Blucher on horseback in the centre being guided by the figure of Victory. The two generals are in Roman military uniforms and Wellington is galloping ahead, with Blucher rushing to his aid; above them Jupiter is riding in a four-horse chariot, a *quadriga*, and hurling a thunderbolt at a circle of giants. The medal has a diameter of 5.3 in.

A fascinating medal, which unscrewed to reveal thirteen miniature coloured pictures of Wellington's victories from 1808 to 1815, was issued in the year of Waterloo. Its obverse has a portrait of Wellington with the inscription 'England's greatest captain, Arthur Duke of Wellington. Porter F'. The reverse has a winged female seated and writing on a tablet 'Record of British valour', with a further inscription 'Picture medal Edwd Orme Direx Bond St London'. Today this medal fetches about £40.

Although American newspapers proclaimed for some time after Waterloo that Napoleon had won the battle, and later claimed that he was coming to America or possibly going to become King of England, the fact remained that he was transported in the *Bellerophon* to St Helena. Webb issued a medal to mark the voyage, showing the bust of Napoleon on the obverse, and two warships on the reverse with the inscription 'Surrendered to HBMS Bellerophon Capt. Maitland. XV July MDCCCXV'. Napoleon died on St Helena in 1821, guarded by 3,000 troops and a squadron of ships.

Chapter Six

The Nineteenth Century

THE ROYAL FAMILY

The nineteenth century saw the issuing of more medals than any other century in British history, and for convenience they will be dealt with by subject in this chapter. Political, military and naval medals connected with the Napoleonic wars have already been covered.

Medals connected with the royal family begin with a number connected with Edward, Duke of Kent, father of Queen Victoria. Struck in copper and white metal in 1819 by W. Wyon, the, link his name with the Lancastrian system of education, begun by Joseph Lancaster to supply primary education to the people. One teacher ran a school of up to 500 children housed in a large hall, and used twelve-year-old monitors to assist him in a regimented system of instruction. One of the medals has the inscription 'Edward, Duke of Kent, friend of education and the soldier's friend', on the obverse, and 'Patron of the Royal Lancastrian System. May heavens blessings long attend his countries glory and its friend', on the reverse. Another describes him as the patron of the system and proclaims him to be 'The wise son of a pious father'.

The coronation medal of George IV by Benedetto Pistrucci was struck in gold, silver and copper. On the obverse appears the laureated head of the king, and on the reverse the winged figure of Victory holding the crown over the seated king, while Britannia, Hibernia and Scotia look on; the inscription in Latin translates 'Henceforth there will be lasting Justice', and the date of the coronation, 19 July 1821, follows. When George's clothes were disposed of after his death in 1830 for £30,000, no less than £10,000 in notes was found in the pockets. His rejection of his wife Caroline, and her attempt to gain admission to the coronation, are the subject of sympathetic medals. P. Kempson struck one in white metal showing her wearing pearls in her hair and inscribed, 'Caroline D G Britt Regina' on the obverse; and, on the reverse, a ship sailing towards Britannia, who is holding out a wreath, with the words 'Hail Britain's Queen! Thy virtues we acknowledge and lament thy wrongs. Returned to England, June 5, 1820'. Another, struck in copper and white metal has her portrait on the obverse with the words 'Caroline Regina born 17 May 1768. MDCCCXX'; on the reverse the queen and her lady-in-waiting are landing from a boat to the cheers of a group, while cannons salute her, and the inscription reads 'Restored to the country'.

Two struck in white metal in 1821 continue the sad tale. The first shows her with an unhappy face, wearing a large feathered hat and high collar, with the words, 'Caroline the injured Queen of England' on the obverse, and an angel greeting and crowning her on the reverse, together with the inscription 'Denied on earth bestow'd in heaven, Augt VII 1821'. The second has her portrait on the obverse, and a tomb with trees round it on the reverse; the tomb is inscribed 'Died Aug 7, 1821, aet.33', while below is written 'Here persecutions victim sleeps at peace where tyrants vex not and the weary rest'.

The coronation of William IV was marked by a medal issued in gold, silver and copper by William Wyon. The obverse has the bare head of the king and the words 'William the fourth crowned Sep 8 1831. W Wyon'; the reverse shows the queen, 'Adelaide, queen consort, crowned Sep 8 1831. W Wyon'. William IV once gave a course of lectures on adultery to the House of Lords! Pistrucci struck the gold, silver and copper medal for Victoria's coronation. The queen's head is done in high relief on the obverse. The reverse shows the figures of Anglia, Scotia and Hibernia offering the crown to the queen, seated before a lion; the Latin inscription translates 'You will have a celebrated reign'.

Victoria's visits to places were often marked by the issue of medals. For example in 1849 she visited Ireland in the royal paddle-steamer; the *Illustrated London News* expressed the fear that she would only see the triumphal arches and none of Ireland's miseries, though it did record that the Lord Lieutenant ordered a dinner for 1,000 poor people in Dublin. The medal commemorating the visit has the conjoined busts of Victoria and Albert on the obverse, and an Irish harp surmounted by a crown on the reverse, with the words 'Every heart throbs with hope of the future. The first visit of a British Queen to Ireland, Augt. 1849'. In 1851 she visited Manchester, arriving in Lord Ellesmere's barge on the Bridgewater Canal, but it rained when she went on to Peel Park to meet 800,000 children and 4,000 teachers. The commemorative medal has the crowned queen on the obverse, and a view of Manchester across a river bridge on the reverse; the inscription reads 'In commemoration of the visit of her most gracious majesty Queen Victoria & H.R.H. Prince Albert to Manchester, 10 Octr. 1851—John Potter Esq. Mayor. J.C. Grundy D., Allen & Moore F'.

The Prince of Wales's recovery from typhoid in 1872 was marked by a number of medals. W. J. Taylor's in white metal has a view of St Paul's Cathedral on the obverse, and on the reverse, the inscription 'St Paul's Cathedral Feb 27, 1872, national thanksgiving for the recovery of H.R.H. the Prince of Wales'. The London Corporation ordered the striking of a medal showing the prince being blessed while Britannia stands with bowed head; the inscription reads 'I was glad when they said unto me let us go into the House of the Lord'. The reverse shows the interior of the cathedral, the congregation standing as the procession enters; two pillars are engraved with the words 'For the recovery of H.R.H. Prince of Wales, St. Paul's London' and 'National Thanksgiving, 27 Feb 1872'.

Victoria's Golden Jubilee was marked by a medal from A. Scharff. On the obverse are two portraits of the queen, one marking her accession and the other her jubilee. On the reverse Britannia in a chariot is being pulled by two lions led by a genius holding the torch of progress; Justice and Wisdom are in attendance, and a globe completes the picture; the inscription reads 'Annus Jubilaeus 1887'. Well over 100 other medals marked the occasion, and in 1897 some eighty medals commemorated her Diamond Jubilee. The finest bore an 1837 Wyon portrait of the queen on the reverse, and an 1897 portrait by Sir Thomas Brock, engraved by de Saulles, on the obverse. It was struck in 2in and 1in sizes and in gold, silver and bronze, a grand total of 338,295 being issued.

POLITICAL AFFAIRS

The use of political commemorative medals was common in the nineteenth century. Dissatisfaction with the corrupt electoral system is expressed on some medals. In 1811 a white-metal medal was issued with an oak-leaf border on the obverse bearing the words 'Sir Berkeley William Guise Bart and the independent electors of the county of Gloucester AD 1811', and on the reverse 'May the spirit of British freedom protect the elective franchise from the corruptions of aristocracy'. The notoriously corrupt borough of Gloucester, where the freeman-franchise was the subject of Parliamentary investigation at least once during the century, witnessed the issuing of a white-metal medal with an oak-leaf garland and the inscriptions 'Colonel Webb and the independent electors of the city of Gloucester AD 1816' on the obverse, and 'May the spirit of freedom protect the elective franchise from the corruption of an overwhelming ministerial faction', on the reverse. The Whig Webb defeated the Tory Cooper by 119 votes on the last day of a seven-day poll after polling the same number of votes as his opponent for the first five days. In Evesham a copper medal was struck showing the bell tower, and inscribed 'The right of election is in the mayor, aldermen capital and other burgesses, members of the corporation' on the obverse, and on the reverse 'This medal is presented by Sir Charles Cockerell, Baronet, to the burgesses of Evesham, members of the corporation, in commemoration of the triumph of justice and independence obtained by his exertions, in support of their petition before the honourable House of Commons on the 23 of February 1819'.

The Peterloo Massacre of 1819 was the subject of an anonymous copper medal showing a fierce fight in progress, cavalrymen sabring a man, woman and children; the inscription reads 'Manchester August 16 1819'. The reverse reads 'The wicked have drawn out the sword. They have cut down the poor and needy and such as be of upright conversation, Psalm XXXVII XIV'.

Political agitation for Parliamentary reform came from places like Birmingham, which had no MPs, and the formation of the Birmingham Political Union under middle-class leadership led to the issue of a white-metal medal with a crown spreading its rays like a sun, and a motto reading 'Unity, Liberty, Prosperity', together with the inscription, 'God save the King 25 January 1830,

Page 176, Nineteenth Century (I)
(1) J. Bellingham executed, 1812; (2) Evesham election, 1819; (3) Peterloo Massacre, 1819; (4) Lichfield election, 1830; (5) Reform Bill, 1832.

Birm. Political Union', on the obverse. The reverse bears a lion and
the words 'The safety of the King & of the people. The Constitution
nothing less and nothing more'. The 'father' of Political Unions,
Thomas Attwood, was the subject of two medals. The first had his
portrait on the obverse and the words 'Thomas Attwood, Esq.
Founder of Political Unions', while on the reverse was the inscription
'The uncompromising enemy of corruption, and unwearied supporter
of Parliamentary reform, whose counsels, incorruptible integrity,
and devotion to his country's weal have endeared him to every
friend of rational freedom'. The second, struck in white metal by
J. Davis, has a lion and a portrait of Attwood on the obverse, and
the words 'The purity of the constitution. Founder of the Political
Unions, The peace & safety of the Kingdom'. The reverse has a
dove, fasces and the head of Prime Minister Earl Grey, with the
motto 'Unity, Liberty, Prosperity', and the inscription 'Chipping
Norton Political Union established Nov 23, 1831. The Reform Bill
nothing less'.

The demand for Parliamentary reform is reflected in a Lichfield
election medal of 1830 which was struck by Ottley. The inscription
on the obverse reads: 'Lichfield election 1830 King and Constitution
The True Blue interest for ever', and that on the reverse: 'The free
and unbought electors who voted for Sir E Dolman Scott Bart'.
Scott was a Whig Reformer who was supported by the Tories as well
as the Whigs, but he only polled 238 votes and lost the election to
Sir George Anson (300 votes) and George Vernon (280 votes), two
Whigs who opposed Parliamentary reform and had used their
power to sway the voters. At the next election in 1831 Anson and
Scott were both elected.

The Reform Bill of 1832 attracted a number of medals, three of
which will be considered here. The first, struck in copper and
white metal, has the inscription 'Patron HMGM William IV Rex.
Earl Grey, Lord Brougham, Lord John Russell and the people,
1831' on the obverse. On the reverse in a centre circle is the word
'Reform', and radiating from it the words, 'England, Scotland,
Ireland, Wales, the Church, the Aristocracy, the boroughmongers,
the public, expenditure, the army, the navy, corporations, taxations,
corn laws, slavery, immorality, monopolies, bank charter, India
charter, the colonies, the currency, representation'; encircling the

whole is the inscription, 'The Rights of the People. Commerce, trade, cheap bread, happiness'. When the bill was passed, Davis produced a celebratory copper medal showing the king on a high throne, crowned and reading a proclamation, with gentlemen in attendance on his left and Britannia and a lion on his right; the inscription reads 'Our cause hath triumphed gloriously, the horse & his rider hath he thrown into the sea, Exodus Chap 15 v 21'. The reverse is inscribed with a detailed table of the votes cast at each stage of the bill, with the words 'Ministerial Bill of Reform introduced by L J Russel Mar 1 1831. Royal assent June 7 1832, Earl Grey and his ministers resigned May 8 1832, reappointed May 15, 1832'. Halliday's medal for the occasion has three heads on the obverse named 'Grey, Russel, Brougham', with the words 'The confidence of the people'. The reverse is inscribed 'The desire of the people, the Reform Bill, no tithes, no corn laws, no unmerited pensions, no game laws, no stamp taxes, no East India monopoly, no colonial slavery'.

The agitation against the Corn Laws was marked in 1839 by the anonymous issue of a copper medal depicting a sheaf of corn in the foreground and sacks and a ship in the distance; 'Peace, Plenty, Happiness' reads the inscription. The reverse has a wreath of corn and the blunt inscription 'No Corn Laws'. Peel's repeal of the laws in 1846 led to the striking of a medal in copper and white metal with his bust on the obverse together with two corn sheaves, a cornucopia with fruit tumbling out of it, a barrel and a sack, and the inscription 'To commemorate the passing of Sir Rbt. Peel's Free Trade measures June 25, Royal assent June 26 1846. Allen & Moore Birm'. The reverse has four heads named Cobden, Bright, Wilson and Villiers, all of whom were involved in the repeal, and the words 'Corn Bill passed June 25, 1846. Anti Corn Law League established 1839'.

Daniel O'Connell, the Irish MP who championed his country's struggle in the nineteenth century, was the subject of a number of medals throughout his political life. For example in 1831 Halliday struck a copper medal bearing his bust on the obverse, with the words 'The friend of his country'; and on the reverse a harp, together with a lengthy inscription claiming him to be 'the enlightened friend of his country's rights, the virtuous, eloquent undaunted defender'. The expedition of Ulstermen who went to the rescue of

Page 179, The Nineteenth Century (II)

(1) Queen Caroline, 1820; (2) Plymouth Regatta, 1820; (3) Peel's Free Trade, 1846; (4) Rev Theobald Mathew, 1838; (5) 'Great Britain under the dominion of the Church of Rome,' 1850.

Captain Boycott in 1880 was the subject of a white-metal medal engraved on the obverse 'The Boycott Expedition Lough Mask, 1880. William Manning Combination, Somerset H Maxwell, Norris Goddard', and, on the reverse 'In honour of the loyal & brave Ulstermen', with a crown. Lough Mask was the name of Boycott's home, and Manning was a Dublin gentleman who had written to the Dublin *Express* signing himself 'Combination' and calling for the paper to start a subscription to raise £500, so that he could organise an expedition to go and gather Boycott's harvest, which his tenants had refused to do. Captain Maxwell, the local Conservative candidate, and Goddard, a Dublin solicitor, came to Manning's aid. The money was easily forthcoming. Manning proposed to lead 100 men armed with Remington rifles to Lough Mask by special train, but the government intervened and allowed him to take only fifty men armed with revolvers by ordinary train, though heavily protected by troops. The *Express* gave the expedition eight days' supplies of food and whisky. Its members camped at Lough Mask for a fortnight and gathered in the harvest in spite of heavy rain and snow. Michael Davitt reckoned that it cost £3,500 to harvest Boycott's £350 crop.

Gladstone was of course featured in various medals during his career. T. J. Minton struck a white metal one carrying his portrait on the obverse, and on the reverse the inscription 'In commemoration of Mr Gladstone's candidature for south west Lancashire, 1868'. L. C. Wyon of the Royal Mint produced a high-relief portrait of Gladstone at the age of seventy; the inscription '29 December 1879 Liverpool' appeared on the reverse, together with a passage from one of Horace's Odes which translates, 'May you return late to heaven and may you remain happy for a long time among your people'. Liverpool was Gladstone's birthplace.

WAR AND MUTINY

The Crimean War offered medallists the usual opportunities, Allen and Moore striking a medal in copper and white metal to mark the alliance between England and France. On the obverse are a grenadier and a French soldier, arm in arm, standing before a cannon, flags and a drum; it is inscribed 'The Holy Alliance, La Sainte Alliance, 1854'. On the reverse is a wreath with the words

'England and France united to defend the oppressed, and avenge insulted Europe'. J. Pinches struck a medal in copper and white metal to record the success of the first battle of the war at the River Alma. Its obverse has an officer, holding a flag and a sword, encouraging his men, with the inscription 'September 20, 1854, Alma'. On the reverse is a long list of the regiments involved. No food or transport arrangements had been made for the troops when they arrived at Eupatoria and they had had to capture 1,000 cattle and sheep and 350 carts before they could proceed to the river.

The charge of the Light Brigade at Balaclava is recorded on a white-metal medal, which shows the cavalry charging at the Russian infantry, with cannon in the foreground; it is inscribed 'Balaclava'. The reverse has a long list of the regiments involved, together with the date, 25 October 1854. The Russian attack on Inkerman, driven off on 5 November, was the subject of another of Pinches' medals, struck in copper and white metal. The obverse shows the infantry using bayonets and the butt ends of their rifles, and is inscribed 'Inkerman'. The reverse gives the date and lists the regiments that took part, their names being written along the rays of a sun, which forms the design of the medal. The year-long siege of Sebastopol is the subject of two interesting medals. The first, by Blachere, has an embossed map marking and naming the troops' positions on the obverse; and the inscription 'Siege de Sebastopol par les armees Francaise, Anglaise et Turque, 1854–1855' on the reverse. The second medal, by W. J. Taylor, shows a view up the estuary with ships, and is inscribed 'Sebastopol, Presented by Underwood & Company first class tea dealers, High St Boro'. The reverse has three soldiers—a grenadier, a Frenchman and a Turk—jumping up with flags on to the wall, and an inscription 'United thus what foe have we to fear'.

Of those who brought comfort to the troops only Florence Nightingale had her work marked by the issue of one of Pinches' medals. It depicts a female reading with bowed head, and is simply inscribed 'Florence Nightingale'. The reverse shows a cross, and a crown lettered 'VR' and surrounded by a garter bearing the words 'Blessed are the merciful', over the word 'Crimea'; the whole is completed with the inscription 'As a mark of esteem and gratitude

Page 182, The Nineteenth Century (III)—Transport
(1) Sheerness Docks, 1823; (2) Gloucester-Berkeley Canal, 1827; (3) Tees Navigation, 1831; (4) *Great Britain*, 1843; (5) *Great Eastern*, 1860.

for her devotion to the Queen's brave soldiers'. Her work had reduced the death rate from 420 per 1,000 to 22.

Pinches recorded the Indian Mutiny with a medal struck in white metal showing a winged laureated female holding a sword by the blade and looking towards rays of light inscribed 'Justice'; behind her is a dead animal and a cannon. The reverse has an oak leaf wreath and the words 'Dedicated to the brave defenders of our Indian Empire during the Sepoy mutinies AD MDCCCLVII'.

The death of General Gordon in 1885 was marked by the issue of a copper medal with his bust on the obverse, and the inscription 'In memory of "Chinese" Gordon', on the reverse. The medal was designed by McGillivray. Gordon had served in China during his career.

The Boer War at the turn of the century was the subject of a number of medals. Myers Brothers, South African jewellers, produced a white-metal medal. The design on the obverse shows a flagpole with a crown on top, a sailor standing to attention beside it, armed with a rifle, and, behind him, a field gun and ship; on the other side of the flagpole is a soldier wearing a pith-helmet and holding his rifle at the ready, behind him a gun and a bell tent. The inscription reads 'Transvaal Souvenir, 1899–1900, the Queen, God bless her'. On the reverse is a crown, the royal arms, and the Transvaal coat of arms, with the motto 'We serve under one crown. United in the cause of freedom we defend our people'. Spinks issued a medal in both copper and white metal with the bust of Baden-Powell wearing his 'Boy Scout' hat and holding binoculars, on the obverse, and on horseback on the reverse, where he is escorted by a sailor holding a Union Jack and a pith-helmeted soldier as they pass a field gun, beside which a soldier is waving his hat in the air. The inscription reads 'Mafeking, 1899–1900'. A similar medal, with the bust of Lord Roberts instead of Baden-Powell on the obverse, and the same scene on the reverse, with the inscription '1900, Bloemfontein, Pretoria', was also issued. The ending of the war was marked by a medal depicting a Boer farmer, wearing bandolier and broad-brimmed hat, holding a flag and pointing to the lion of England to leave; the inscription is a plain 'Hands off. 1902'. On the reverse are the bearded busts of Christian de Wet and Koos de la Rey.

DOMESTIC AND TRANSPORT ACHIEVEMENTS

Agriculture is represented by countless prize medals presented at agricultural shows, but these fall outside the scope of this book. There is one curious white-metal medal, however, which presents something of a mystery. Struck in 1846, its obverse has a large triangle along whose sides are written 'Love supersedes self interest—interest, capitalists, money', 'Age regulates advantages—profit, labourers, labour', and 'Rent, landlords, rent'. Outside the triangle is written 'Edward King's Triform System of Colonization, 1846. Love one another or you will torment one another, seek bliss not riches'. The reverse has a circular plan of a settlement dissected by four roads named North, South, East and West; the segments between them are divided up, and named from the outer rim inwards 'Farmyards', '25 orchards each 100 yards long', and '25 flower gardens each 50 yards long'. Who King was and why he produced his plan remains something of a mystery. There was a man named King working as bailiff of the Chartist Land Company in connection with its agricultural settlements at Snigs End and Lowbands in Gloucestershire, and it may be that he devised his own ideas as to how such settlements should work. The Chartist attempts at transforming factory workers into agriculturalists were disastrous failures, for they expected the settlers to be superhuman farmers, producing as much from an acre as a farmer got from 100 acres.

In 1856 the Royal Agricultural Society of England held its first show at Chelmsford, and what the *Illustrated London News* described as the first medal ever issued for such an occasion was designed by Harrison Weir for J. Pinches in white metal. The obverse has a bull in the foreground, with horses and sheep behind and a plough below; the inscription reads 'To commemorate the visit of the Royal Agricultural Society of England'. The reverse has a picture of the County Hall, Chelmsford.

The earliest transport medals in the nineteenth century were, interestingly, those connected with flying. In 1811 a medal was struck in copper and white metal with the semi-bald head of a man whom the inscription describes as 'James Sadler first English Aeronaut'. The reverse shows a balloon with a highly ornamented basket containing two persons and two flags; the inscription reads 'The 21 Ascent October 7, 1811, ascended from Birmingham travers'd upwards of 112 miles in 1 hour & 20 minutes'. Sadler had made his first ascent in 1784, and after a number of hair-raising trips had abandoned his attempts until 1810, when he took up the 'sport' again. On this particular trip a Mr Burcham accompanied him and the balloon was swept along by a gale, which resulted in the fastest journey mankind had performed at that time! When he tried to land in Lincolnshire, he was thrown out, leaving his passenger to fly on for another 1½ miles until the balloon was torn to pieces in an ash tree. Each believed the other dead until they met in the village of Heckington.

In 1837 W. J. Taylor struck a white-metal medal bearing the head of Charles Green, the aeronaut, on the obverse, and a balloon flying over a town on the reverse, a river and bridge also being visible. The inscription reads 'From London November 7, 1836, in company with Robt Hollond MP & M Mason Esq to Weilburg Germy in 18 hours'. Travelling in his £500 *Royal Vauxhall* balloon with the MP and Monck Mason, a distinguished flute player, Green left Vauxhall at 1.30 pm. The crimson and white balloon was cemented together instead of sewn and had a capacity of 70,000 cu ft. Its basket was 9 ft by 4 ft and had eagles' heads at both ends. For the first time a trail rope was fitted to act as an automatic height regulator. Their stores included a coffee heater, which worked on quicklime, 40 lb of meat, 45 lb of preserves and fowls, 40 lb of bread, biscuit and sugar, 2 gal sherry, 2 gal port and 2 gal brandy. The balloon passed Dover Castle at 4.48 pm and continued across the Channel at 25 mph. Green knocked the coffee heater overboard in the darkness, and when dawn came they wondered whether they had reached Russia! They landed at Weilburg at 7.30 am, having done 480 miles in 18 hours, the greatest flight to date. They were entertained for days and the balloon, occupied by Green and eight young ladies, was christened 'The Great Balloon of Nassau', the latter being the duchy in which Weilburg was situated. They then packed the balloon into a secondhand carriage drawn by four horses and set off through torrential rain to Paris, where it was exhibited.

The long-awaited opening of the Gloucester-Berkeley Canal in 1827 was marked by a bronze and white metal medal by T. Halliday, showing a three-masted ship on the obverse, with the inscription

Page 186, The Nineteenth Century (IV)—Transport
(1) Railway bridge at Newton, 1830; (2) Sankey Viaduct, 1830;
(3) Liverpool Station and tunnel, 1830; (4) Stockton-Darlington Railway,
1830; (5) Timetable of miles from Birmingham, 1837

'Gloucester & Berkeley Canal commenced 1793'. The reverse records 'Resumed under the auspices of his Royal Highness the Duke of Gloucester 15 July AD 1818 and completed 26 April 1827. The 16 mile canal was opened with due ceremony, a band being hired for ten guineas and the local bell-ringers being paid £2 3s od. A procession of boats passed down the canal to the accompaniment of gunfire, but the guests on board were disappointed that no luncheon was supplied. Financial problems had delayed the canal's completion for years. Most of the work had been done by a work force of 971 men, but in 1796 a machine was introduced and aroused wonder by removing 1,400 loaded barrows from the bottom of the canal to a distance of 40 ft in 12 hours, while operated by only two men.

The coming of the railways resulted in the striking of a number of fascinating medals. In 1830 T. W. Ingram produced a white-metal medal showing five ships unloading at coal lifts with the inscription 'Stockton & Darlington Railway Cos. coal staiths at Middlesbro', on the obverse, and a view through an arch to the far end of a bridge under which a ship is sailing on the reverse, together with the inscription 'Suspension bridge near Stockton Middlesbro' branch railway opened Dec 27,1830'. When the line was opened, the company operated it like a turnpike, charging for any vehicles that used it. This caused considerable timetable difficulties when steam trains competed with horse drawn carriages, and finally the company began operating the line itself.

The same year saw the striking of three medals to mark the opening of the Liverpool & Manchester Railway. The first has the head of George Stephenson on the obverse, and a goods train crossing a viaduct with the words 'Bridge at Newton, Liverpool & Manchester Railway opened Sept. 15, 1830', on the reverse. A Mr Prentice noted that the fact that a million people would cross the bridge a year, and so see the hitherto unseen village of Newton, would convince them of 'the absurdity of its sending two members to Parliament whilst Manchester sends none'. He was right, for the 1832 Reform Act took away the village's members. Ottley of Birmingham produced a copper medal with a goods train going over a viaduct with the words 'Viaduct over the Sankey Canal & valley 14½ miles from Liverpool. G Stephenson Esq

Page 188, The Nineteenth Century (V)
(1) Thames Tunnel, 1842; (2) Menai
Bridge, 1850; (3) Crystal Palace, 1851;
(4) Edward King's Triform Colonisation,
1846; (5) Royal Agricultural Society of
England, Chelmsford, 1856.

engineer', on the obverse, and, on the reverse, inside a wreath, the inscription 'The Liverpool and Manchester Railroad this grand national undertaking had the royal assent April 12, 1827—opened September 15, 1830 in the presence of his grace the Duke of Wellington and other distinguished personages'. Halliday produced a medal in copper and white metal with the viaduct on the obverse and the words 'Viaduct over the Sankey Canal & valley to commemorate the opening of the Liverpool and Manchester railroad Sept. 15 1830'. The reverse shows a station, a tunnel entrance with three trains on the tracks, and 'Entrance to the Liverpool station & tunnels. Published by T Woolfield, Bazaar, Liverpool'.

The tunnel bored under Liverpool was the first great railway tunnel and it partially caved in during its construction so that the 300 miners had to be chivvied back to work. They dug the $1\frac{1}{4}$ mile tunnel by candlelight and visitors sometimes descended the 60 ft shafts in a bucket to see them at it. The nine-arch Sankey viaduct was described by the Duke of Wellington at the opening as 'stupendous' and 'magnificent'.

The opening of the Grand Junction Railway was marked by a white-metal medal designed by T. Halliday, which shows a large colonnaded building on the obverse, described as the 'Grand facade of the New Railway Station Liverpool'. On the reverse trains travel in opposite directions on a viaduct, while ships sail beneath it and cows graze in the fields; the inscription reads 'Viaduct over the valley of the Weaver published to commemorate the opening of the Grand Junction Railway July 4, 1837, by W B Promoli, late Thos Woolfield, Church Street, Liverpool'. An anonymously issued white-metal medal shows two viaducts converging in the distance, with lines marked to Birmingham, London, Liverpool and Lawley Street, and the inscription 'Birmingham, Liverpool & Manchester Grand Junction Railway begun 1835, opened July 4, 1837, cost L.1,500,000. J Locke Engr.' The reverse has the company's timetable:

Miles from Birm. and Time in going.

	Miles	H	M
W–Hampton	$14\frac{1}{2}$	0	40
Stafford	$29\frac{1}{2}$	1	15
Whitmore	$43\frac{1}{4}$	1	55
Crewe	54	2	24

	Miles	H	M
Hartford	$65\frac{3}{4}$	2	59
Warrington	78	3	34
Manchester	$97\frac{1}{4}$	4	30
Liverpool	$97\frac{1}{4}$	4	30

Travels the whole distance in $4\frac{1}{2}$ H.

Around this table is inscribed '1st class leaves Manchester & Liverpool at $\frac{1}{2}$ pt 6, $\frac{1}{2}$ pt 1 am & $\frac{1}{2}$ pt 2 & $\frac{1}{2}$ pt 6 pm'.

Medals were also struck in connection with the London-Birmingham Railway (1838), the Edinburgh-Glasgow Railway (1842), the Newcastle-Carlisle Railway (1844) and the Chester-Holyhead Railway (1850).

Ships and shipwrecks were also the subject of commemorative medals. In 1839 W. Wyon produced a medal in both silver and copper for the Liverpool Shipwreck Society, which had been founded in that year after a hurricane had destroyed many lives. It aimed to provide money for bereaved relatives and to reward bravery in lifesaving. The medal has a liver bird within an oak wreath and the inscription 'Liverpool Shipwreck and Humane Society 1839', on the obverse, and a shipwreck scene with the words 'Lord save us we perish', on the reverse.

The launching of the *Great Britain* in 1843 was marked by Allen & Moore of Birmingham with a copper medal that has the queen's and Prince Albert's busts on the obverse, and the ship with its one funnel and six masts in full sail on the reverse, with the inscription '*The Great Britain*, length 322 ft, breadth 50 ft 6 in, depth 32 ft 6 in. 26 staterooms with 1 bed e^h 113 with 2 beds e^h. Total wht of iron 1,500 tns. 1,000 horse power. Launched by HRH Prince Albert July 19, 1843'. A pewter medal was also struck, its obverse similar to the reverse of the first medal, but with the additional words 'Built by the Great Western Steam Ship Company'. The reverse consists of a long inscription referring to an experimental voyage to test the strength of its iron hull: 'River Thames, Jan. 26, 1845. We, the undersigned passengers, on board "The Great Britain" steam ship, on her experimental voyage from Bristol to London, having witnessed her performance during a stiff gale and a heavy sea, do express our conviction of her great length being no detriment to her excellent sailing qualities and her sea worthiness and of the great advantage of the application of Mr. Smith's screw, as also our sense of the skill, attention and urbanity of her Commandant, Lieut. Hosken, R.N.' This statement was followed by the names of twenty-five persons. Mr Smith was Francis Pettit Smith, who had patented his invention of a screw propeller in 1836. The hull was clinker-built of iron plates, 6 ft by 2 ft each. She was the first ship with balanced rudder and bolted rudder post. When the *Great Britain* returned to Bristol in 1970, Overton, Farrel & Sons struck 500 gold and 5,000 silver medals to mark the event. The obverse is similar to Allen & Moore's medal, while the reverse is inscribed 'To commemorate the safe return of *SS Great Britain* to Bristol on 19 July 1970'.

Brunel's *Great Eastern* was the subject of two medals. A white-metal medal struck in 1859 has the bust of Brunel on the obverse, giving the dates of his birth and death (1806–59), and on the reverse is the four-funnelled, six-masted paddle steamer and the inscription '*The Great Eastern* Steam Ship, screw, paddle and sail, four decks, would accomodate 10,000 troops, 696f long, 35 f wide, height of hull 60 f, 24,000 tons burden, 2,600 horse power'. The other medal was issued in copper and white-metal and shows the ship on the obverse surrounded by smaller boats and watched by cheering crowds. The reverse inscription reads 'Purchased on Board the *Great Eastern* 1860. Tonage 24,000. Horsepower 2,600. Length 692 ft. Breadth 83 ft. Depth 60 ft.' When it was launched in 1859 the *Illustrated London News* recalled the fears of its impracticality and pointed out that it proved its strength when the launching cradles jammed and a large part of the ship was left in the air unsupported, for no cracks appeared. It was speculated that the ship would do the trip to Calcutta in thirty-two days without refueling.

A major safety measure for shipping was the introduction of the Plimsoll Line, painted on the side of ships to indicate the maximum load they could carry. This was the result of Samuel Plimsoll, MP, losing his temper with the Commons, which had repeatedly ignored him, and shouting 'You're a lot of damned murderers'. The outcome was a medal struck in brass and bronze with the words, 'S. Plimsoll House of Commons 22 July 1875 London', on the obverse, and a sinking ship with a skull and crossbones on its sail, labelled 'Coffin Ship', on the reverse. The latter name was given to overloaded ships, on which owners knew they could claim insurance if they sank.

The nineteenth century was justly proud of its industrial feats, and many bridges, tunnels and dock schemes were recorded on medals. A typical example is the seven-arched Dunkeld Bridge, which appears on an anonymous medal with the words 'Bridge of Dunkeld length 685 ft Breadth 27 and centre arch is 90 feet'. The reverse has the inscription 'BUILT by the most noble John, Duke of Atholl expence above L30,000, founded 24th June 1805 and open'd the 7th Novr 1808'. Another is that struck in gilt for London Bridge in 1831, which shows the five-arched bridge with ships and is inscribed 'Length 928 ft, width 56 ft, carriageway 36 ft, waterway 692 ft, centre arch 152, side arches 140, extreme 130, height 55'. The reverse has the inscription 'New London Bridge first stone was laid by the Rt Hon the Lord Mayor John Garratt esqr on the 15 June 1825 and the bridge opened by their majesties the 1st Aug 1831 cost 506,000 pounds'. Benjamin Wyon also struck a medal on that occasion, showing the bridge on the reverse, and William IV on the obverse. For the opening ceremony a royal tent was pitched on the London side of the bridge with tables for 164 guests, and a 400 ft awning was stretched along the length of the bridge to cover tables for a further 1,560 guests.

The Menai bridges were the subject of a white-metal medal of 1850, showing the tubular bridge in the foreground, the suspension bridge in the distance, and sailing ships; the inscription reads 'The MENAI SUSPENSION and BRITANNIA TUBULAR BRIDGES'. The reverse was laid out as follows:

Details of the Bridges

Suspension	Tubular
Total length 910 ft	Total length of tubes 1513 ft
Height of Roadway	Height above high
above high water 100 ft	water 102 ft
Height of the two	Height of the two
main pillars 153 ft	Land Towers 203 ft
Suspended weight	do centre towers 221 ft
of iron 489 tns	Weight of each of
Total weight	the four large
of iron 2186 tns	tubes 1800 tns
Extreme	do small tubes 700 tns
length of chain 1714 ft	Total weight 10,000 tns

Published by J. A. Ronson, Bangor.

When Queen Victoria opened Blackfriars Bridge in 1869, the Lord Mayor ordered the striking of a copper medal, to be sold in a blue morocco case lined with red velvet and white satin. The obverse has the queen wearing a coronet, while the reverse has Holborn Viaduct at the top, Blackfriars Bridge below, St Paul's behind and a paddle steamer in the foreground; the City Arms are in the centre, together with a female holding a scroll inscribed 'opened Nov 6', and Britannia.

Gilt and white-metal versions of the medal marking the opening of Tower Bridge were struck in 1894. The obverse has the busts of the Prince of Wales and Princess Alexandra, and the reverse a long inscription:

> The Tower Bridge of London opened June 30, 1894 by their R.H. the Prince and Princess of Wales. The bridge was commenced in 1886 & finished 1894 & the cost of it is over a million. Length of Bridge with approaches is half a mile. The high level spans are 142 feet above high water. The shore spans are 270 feet & the middle one 200 feet long. The bascules weigh 950 tons each. The lead ballast on the short leg weighs 290 tons. The main pivots through each of the bascules are 21 inch steel bars & bears above a thousand tons. The lifts will take 30 people at a go. What was used in the making of the tower bridge: 20,000 tons of cement & Portland stone. 70,000 cubic yards of concrete, 14,000 tons of steel & about 2,000,000 rivets have been used. 500 to 800 men have been generally at work on it. The Tower Bridge is a steel structure & trimmed with stone.

W. J. Taylor produced medals in copper and white metal to mark the opening of Brunel's Thames Tunnel in 1842. On the obverse is the head of Brunel; on the reverse is a steamship with masts rigged for sails proceeding down river, while below it the twin tunnels are shown in section. Another white-metal medal by Davis of Birmingham shows a close view of the twin tunnels and the inscription 'Rotherhithe Entrance Thames tunnel 12000 feet long, commenced 1824, completed 1842. 76 feet below high water. Cost L450,000. Sir I M Brunel engineer'. Other medals struck on the occasion have the tunnel on one side and the names of the directors or the heads of Victoria and Albert on the other. Seven men had died on the job and many had been overcome by the bad air as they worked behind the boring 'shield'.

A white-metal medal recorded the dockyard developments at

Sheerness, with an 'aerial' plan of the improvements and the inscription 'Basin and docks at Sheerness begun January XIX MDCCCXIV, opened September V MDCCCXXIII'. The reverse is plain. The enlargement of the dockyard had become necessary to cope with the navy's increased demands and the work was designed and carried out by Sir John Rennie at a cost of £1,616,757. In 1831 W. A. Brooks issued a copper medal to mark the Tees improvements. The obverse has a sailing ship and an inscription reading 'Tees Navigation Compy incorporated by Act of Parlt 1808. New channel opened 27 Sept 1810 Meliora speramus'. The reverse shows three sailing ships passing along the channel against a hilly background, and is inscribed 'In commemoration of the opening of the New Channel to Newport on the 10 Feby 1831 and other improvements for deepening & straightening the rest of the channel of the river between Stockton & the sea'.

In 1858 A. Aston struck a white-metal medal for the Newport dock extension. The obverse shows two interconnected docks with sailing ships, and the town, and has an inscription reading 'Length 950 ft, Breadth 350 ft, Depth 26 ft. Cost £64,000. Area of new & old docks 57,000 yds'. The reverse is inscribed 'In commemoration of the opening of the Newport dock extension March 2, 1858', followed by a list of persons involved in the work.

Piers were sometimes the subject for medals: in 1823 B. Wyon struck a bronze one for Brighthelmstone Pier, with the head of George III on the obverse and the pier on the reverse with the inscription 'Brighthelmstone Royal Pier designed & erected by Samuel Brown Esq: Commander in His Majesty's Navy 1823'. Regattas also found their medallists: T. W. Ingram struck a gilt medal for the Plymouth Regatta of 1820 which shows sailing ships and rowing fours crossing the bay on the reverse, and a crowned Neptune holding his trident as he skims across the water in a three-horse chariot on the obverse; and W. Taylor issued a white-metal medal with the two heads of Isis and Tamesis on the obverse, and a wreath inscribed 'Henley Regatta established 1839' on the reverse.

Nelson's memorial, Trafalgar Square, is recalled by W. Griffin (London) on a white-metal medal showing the bust of Nelson on the obverse, and the square on the reverse with the inscription

'The Nelson Column Trafalgar Squ^r London. Teneriffe, Copenhagen, Nile, Trafalgar. W Railton Arch. 1843'. Sometimes a medal recorded destruction rather than construction. An 1844 gilt medal shows a four-storeyed building on the obverse with the inscription 'Formerly the Red Lion Public House West St Smithfield'; the reverse records 'The resort of the notorious housebreaker Jack Sheppart and other noted characters pulled down Augt 12 1844'.

Exhibitions were the subject of medals, too, and those connected with the Great Exhibition of 1851 will serve as an example. The aim of the exhibition was brought out by Ottley of Birmingham's white-metal medal depicting Britannia surrounded by ships, a train, a cogwheel and a globe, on the reverse, and with the heads of the Queen and Prince Albert and a view of the Crystal Palace, on the obverse, with the words 'Exhibition of industry of all nations, London, 1851—proposed by HRH Prince Albert, designed by Joseph Paxton esqre F.L.S., erected by Fox Henderson & Co'. Another medal struck in copper and white metal has the Crystal Palace on the obverse with the inscription 'The Crystal Palace designed by Mr Paxton for the Great Exhibition in London, 1851'. The reverse records its dimensions: 'Height 1848 ft, width 408 ft, height of roof 66ft, height of transept 103 ft, glazed surface 900,000 ft; 18 acres; cost £150,000'. The interior is depicted on a white-metal medal showing the trees inside it and people looking at the exhibits, with the words 'Interior view of the Crystal Palace London 1851'. The reverse records: 'This unique structure has 3320 cast iron columns, 358 wrought iron trusses, 8 miles of exhib^n tables, 34 miles of gutters, 202 miles of sash bars, 400 tons of glass and cost £150,000'.

One exhibit is featured on a copper medal, which shows a machine with a large wheel and the inscription 'Coining press invented 1817 and made by D Uhlhorn at Grevenbroich near Cologne on the Rhine'; on the reverse is 'Exhibition of the industry of all nations 1851, London', and round the edge 'May industry be crowned with success'. Uhlhorn's was not the only coining press on exhibition, for Maudslay's double-cylinder direct-acting high-pressure press was also on show, claiming a pressure of 140 tons.

Sporting occasions sometimes merited medals and an interesting example is that of a white-metal medal by W. Taylor of London,

Page 196, The Nineteenth Century (VI)

(1) James Sadler, first English aeronaut, 1811; (2) Charles Green, aeronaut, 1837; (3) Siege of Sebastopol, 1854; (4) Battle of Inkerman, 1854; (5) Florence Nightingale, 1854; (6) Baden-Powell at Mafeking, 1899–1900.

showing a horse on the obverse, and the inscription 'Hermit, winner of the Derby May 22 1867 run in a snowstorm', on the reverse. The betting was 100 to 1 against 'poor Hermit', which was owned by a Mr Chaplain and ridden by J. Daley. It took half an hour to get the thirty competitors ready due to the snow, and Hermit won by a neck in 2 min 52 sec on Benson's Chronograph.

HUMANITY AND RELIGION

Humanitarian and religious events were of course sometimes marked by the issue of medals. The abolition of slavery in the British Empire in 1834 was recorded by a medal struck in copper and white metal showing slaves dancing round a palm tree with the inscription 'Slavery abolished by Great Britain 1834', on the obverse, and the king, seated and attended by four people, announcing 'I advocate this Bill as a measure of humanity', on the reverse. Children in all the Tewkesbury schools were presented with a celebratory medal (with a suspension hole); on the obverse a slave is raising his arms to heaven in gratitude, while holding a broken chain, and in the background are palm trees, a hut and a tobacco plant, with the inscription 'This is the Lord's doing. Psalm 118 v 23. Jubilee Aug 1 1834'. The reverse reads: 'In commemoration of the extinction of colonial slavery throughout the British dominions in the reign of William IV Aug 1 1834. Davis Birm'. An accompanying leaflet said: 'Negro Emancipation. This Medal is most respectfully dedicated to T F Buxton, Esq MP and several of the Members of the Committees of the Anti-Slavery Societies by their obedient servant Joseph Davis'.

The year 1850 was marked by three interesting religious medals. W. J. Taylor produced a copper medal with the head of Lorenzo Snow, 'an apostle of the Church of Jesus Christ of Latter day Saints', on the obverse, and, on the reverse, a star-encircled inscription reading 'List ye nations by this token know that your redemption is nigh 1850'. The decision to establish a Roman Catholic hierarchy in England that year led to the production of the other two medals. One in white metal by Stay of Birmingham shows a bishop on a throne, and before him a table bearing an open book and an inkwell; it is inscribed 'The Bible and the Bible alone is the religion of Protestants. Coverdale, bishop of Exeter, presenting the first

English translation of the Bible. Octr 4th 1535. No Popery, 1850'. On the reverse is a Bible with clasps, chain and padlock, together with the inscription 'Great Britain under the dominion of the Church of Rome. To commemorate the national protest against the appointment of papal hierarchy in England'. In retaliation W. E. Bardells struck a medal bearing the bust of a cardinal on the obverse, and a cardinal's hat and coat of arms on the reverse with the words 'Cardinalis Archiepiscopus Westmonasteriensis Puolaus', a reference to the appointment of Cardinal Wiseman by Pius IX.

Church buildings were occasionally the subject of medals. In 1829 S. Hardy produced a bronze medal showing the exterior of York Minster on the obverse, and the interior of the choir on the reverse with the inscription 'The choir of York Minster destroyed by fire Feb 2nd 1829'. Ottley of Birmingham struck a white-metal medal showing Christ Church, Greton, Gloucestershire on the obverse, and a lengthy inscription on the reverse, reading 'The first stone of this church was laid on the 8 day of April 1867. It was erected to replace the original church which after having been dedicated to the service of God for nearly 600 years, had fallen into decay. Revd J Harvey, vicar of Winchcombe, Revd R Noble Jackson, R N Curate of Greeton & of St Mary's Sudeley Manor, Wm Warder, churchwarden, J Drayton Wyatt, architect, London, Collins & Cullis Builders, Tewkesbury. Consecrated the 4th day of June 1868 by the Right Revd C J Ellicott D.D. Lord Bishop of Gloucester and Bristol'.

In 1838 W. Woodhouse struck a white-metal medal, with a hole for suspension, on behalf of the Cork Temperance Society; it shows the bust of the Rev Theobald Mathew, 'Apostle of Temperance' on the obverse, and, on the reverse, Mathew, dressed in top hat, blessing rows of people who are kneeling before him with the words 'May God bless you and grant you strength and grace to keep your promise'. Father Mathew had succeeded in persuading 2 million people to take the pledge by 1840, but his liabilities amounted to £7,000 and he was arrested because of an outstanding account for medals in 1844. Two dukes, four marquesses, nineteen earls, ten viscounts and barons, four Catholic bishops and thirty MPs presented him with a testimonial and secured him a pension of £300 a year from the British government.

One extraordinary medal will serve to end this chapter. It was struck in 1867 from steel dies that had taken months to cut, and presented by Miss Burdett Coutts to the Acclimatisation of Animals, Birds, Fishes, Insects and Vegetables Society. The obverse has the bearded head of the Prince of Wales, who was the Society's president, together with a wreath of rose, thistle and shamrock. The reverse shows Britannia seated on a rock watching the transmission and exchange of animals (bison, camel, deer, llama, sheep, horse, dog, pheasant, duck, parrot, rabbit), salmon, oysters, insects and vegetables by means of a paddle-steamer in the distance; the inscription simply says 'World Wide'. The medal was to be presented to seafarers who helped the work of the Society.

Chapter Seven

The Twentieth Century

ROYAL OCCASIONS

In contrast to the nineteenth century relatively few commemorative medals have been struck, partly due to the invention of the pictorial and propagandist postage stamp and partly to recurring economic depressions. Fashions change and a wide range of other souvenirs have displaced medals. Signs of a revival are now to be seen, however, and it is interesting to notice that Boots, the chemists, produced medals to mark Prince Charles's investiture as Prince of Wales and the first landing on the moon.

Royal occasions have produced medals on a truly Victorian scale. Edward VII's coronation in 1902 resulted in over 100 medals being struck by a variety of bodies, while de Saulles produced the official medal in three metals and two sizes. On the obverse the crowned and bearded king is pictured with an inscription giving the date of the coronation as 9 August; on the reverse is the crowned portrait of the queen. This coronation was the first to be marked by the issue of medals to be worn by those attending the ceremony, transforming them into 'campaign' medals. George V's coronation in 1911 was marked by forty-two medals; of these, F. Bowcher's, in copper, has the distinction of being the largest coronation medal ever struck. It weighs 16 oz. On the obverse are the conjoined busts of the king and queen, and on the reverse the king being crowned with laurel by Britannia, the queen in attendance. The inscription reads 'Homage of the British Empire, 1911'. In the same year W. G. John struck a medal in gilt, silver and white metal to mark the investiture of the Prince of Wales. The obverse shows the prince dressed in ermine and wearing his coronet, and is inscribed 'Investiture of Edward, Prince of Wales, K.G., Carnarvon July XIII MCMXI'. The reverse has the castle, plus the prince's feathers surmounted by a coronet and the Welsh dragon, and bears the inscription 'Arwisgiad iorwerth tywsog Cymru' ('Investiture of Edward Prince of Wales').

Thirty-six medals were produced for the coronation of Edward VIII, but of course he abdicated before it could take place. They proclaim that he was crowned on 12 May 1937. An official medal was prepared to mark the event, but it was never marketed. On the obverse it carried the crowned portrait of Edward, with the inscription 'His Majesty King Edward VIII'. The reverse had Britannia holding a crown in her right hand and the Union Jack in her left, with a background of St Paul's Cathedral and Blackfriars Bridge seen across water through a large archway; the inscription read 'Crowned A.D. 1937'. The coronation of George VI on 12 May 1937 was marked by a number of medals. One by Percy Metcalfe, produced in three metals, has the crowned portrait of the king on the obverse and the queen on the reverse, together with the date of their coronation. The 'His Master's Voice' record company marked the occasion with a medal issued to radio and gramophone dealers, inscribed 'To commemorate your association with *His Master's Voice* during coronation year 1937'.

The coronation of Elizabeth II in 1953 was marked by relatively few medals, one of which was produced by Pinches, with the bare head of the queen on the obverse and an inscription giving her titles; the reverse shows the crowned queen seated in the stern of a round-ship and three females blowing trumpets, with the inscription 'May its course be prosperous'.

The investiture of Prince Charles as Prince of Wales in 1969 was a heaven-sent opportunity for medallists to come into their own again. The official medal was designed for the Royal Mint by Michael Rizzello and its obverse has the portrait of the prince with the inscription 'Arwisgiad Charles Tywysog Cymru. 1969 Caernarfon' ('Investiture of Charles Prince of Wales. 1969 Caernarvon'). The reverse has the Welsh Dragon and the inscription 'Y Ddraig Gogh ddyry cychwyn' ('The Red Dragon leads the way'). Silver medals struck amounted to 1,500, measuring $2\frac{1}{4}$ in and costing £13 10s each, but they were oversubscribed four times so 7,500 more were struck at the reduced size of 1¾ in for £9 10s. Gilt bronze medals (3,000) at £6 10s each and an unlimited number of 1¼ in bronze ones at £1 17s 6d each were also struck.

A number of investiture medals were issued by private firms. John Pinches offered two, the first in high relief, with oxydised silver finish, carrying a portrait of the prince on the obverse and the inscription 'Investiture of Charles, Prince of Wales, K.G.'; and Caernarvon Castle on the reverse with Welsh Dragon below and the same inscription in Welsh. The second was struck in low relief silver with a portrait of the prince, and inscription 'Charles Prince of Wales', and, on the reverse, the prince's three feathers, with the wording 'Investiture Caernarvon 1969'. Five hundred high relief medals were struck, and 1,000 in low relief. The Mayfair Coin Company struck medals in bronze, oxydised silver and hallmarked silver, bearing a portrait of the prince based on a photograph taken by the royal photographer, Godfrey Argent. The bronze version has the prince's feathers on the reverse, with the inscription 'Investiture Caernarvon Castle 1st July 1969'. The other two have a side view of the Welsh Dragon with a similar inscription. The bronze and oxydised silver issues amounted to 5,000 each, plus 1,000 for the silver.

Geoffrey Hearn of Cork produced a crown-size medal in both gold and silver. The obverse had a portrait of the prince wearing his coronet and prince's robes, and the inscription 'Investiture of Charles Prince of Wales, Caernarvon, July 1969'. The reverse has a view of the castle, with the prince's badge in the sky above and the Welsh Dragon below; the inscription in Welsh proclaims the investiture. Konfax Limited arranged for R. A. McKenzie to design a medal to be struck by Vaughtons of Birmingham in silver and golden bronze. The obverse has a portrait of the prince with the inscription 'Caernarvon Castle. First July 1969. Charles Philip Arthur George'. The reverse has the prince's arms.

The royal visit to New Zealand and Australia in 1970 was marked by the issuing of a bronze medal by the Historical Medal Society of Australia and New Zealand. The obverse bears the royal standard, with a view of land in the distance, and the inscription 'Royal visit to New Zealand March 1970: Australia April 1970'. The reverse is inscribed, 'Her Majesty Queen Elizabeth II, H R H Prince Philip Duke of Edinburgh, H R H Prince Charles Prince of Wales, H R H Princess Anne', above a fern leaf representing New Zealand and a wattle branch Australia, and, round the edge, 'The Historical Medal Society of Australia and New Zealand'.

UNEMPLOYMENT

Back at the beginning of the century, stark reality was recorded by a white-metal medal inscribed 'Leicester Unemployed March to London June 1905'. The reverse is plain. Canon Donaldson had held a church parade and preached that Christ was the leader of the unemployed, and with this thought in mind some 450 men set out to march to London to present their case. Several bands had given them a rousing send-off and bread, cheese and onion rations had been arranged. They averaged 20 miles a day, and half a dozen amateur barbers shaved them before they started. At London they were put up at the Bedford Congregational Chapel, St Pancras. In heavy rain they demonstrated in Hyde Park, with little effect, drying their clothes by the heat of the rubbish-burning furnaces of St Pancras. But a march to St Paul's and Westminster Abbey was watched by thousands, and the Leicester MP, Ramsay MacDonald, spoke in their support; the crowds threw pennies to them. Then began a long hot march home, relieved by the anonymous gift of 150 pairs of boots, 100 coats, 120 shirts and 200 pairs of trousers from a member of the Independent Labour Party. When they arrived home each man was given 3 lb beef, 3 lb potatoes, 1 lb sugar, $\frac{1}{4}$ lb tea and 3 loaves of bread. In addition, the 416 who completed the tramp were presented with medals struck for them on the instructions of Captain Falkiner, headlined as the 'mysterious horseman' who had inspired them throughout their demonstration.

WORLD WAR I

World War I witnessed the striking of a large number of propaganda medals, mostly in Germany. Something like 1,000 were struck as part of the German war effort, ranging from the large *Lusitania* medals to small silver 'Victory Pennies'. The latter were part of a series having a common obverse—the winged figure of Victory and an inscription in German that translates 'God has blessed the

Allied Armies'. The reverses record German victories, like the bombardment of Hartlepool and Scarborough by German ships on 16 December 1914. These medals were very small, about the size of a new penny, and many had suspension loops so that they could be fastened to necklaces or bracelets. In the action referred to above German cruisers killed a number of people at Bridlington and West Hartlepool and broke windows of boarding houses at Scarborough as well as damaging Whitby Abbey.

Karl Goetz was responsible for many of the German medals recording the war against England, one of which was a bronze medal marking the battle of the Falkland Isles on 8 December 1914. The obverse has the busts of three Counts von Spee (Maximilian and his sons Heinrich and Otto); a translation of the inscription reads 'The Counts von Spee; on the *Scharnhorst* the father as admiral, under his command a little squadron; the sons lieutenants, the elder on the *Gneisenau*, the younger on the *Nurnberg*; off the Falkland Isles on the high seas died these German heroes, the three Counts Spee'. The reverse has an eagle flying over the sea near the Falkland Islands, carrying a laurel branch in its talons; it is inscribed '8 December 1914'. Von Spee's squadron had sailed to the Falkland Islands to destroy the British wireless station there, but was surprised by Rear-Admiral Sir Frederick Sturdee's squadron, consisting of the *Invincible, Irresistible, Kent, Cornwall* and *Glasgow*, which outgunned the enemy and sank the *Gneisenau, Scharnhorst, Leipzig* and the *Nurnberg*; only the *Dresden* escaped, but it was sunk later.

The submarine warfare directed against Britain in 1915 was the subject of another of Goetz's bronze medals, on the obverse of which appeared the bust of High Admiral von Tirpitz, and, on the reverse, Neptune, with his trident, seated on the conning tower of a submarine and shaking his fist at two distant British sailing ships, one of which is sinking. The inscription on the reverse reads 'Gott strafe England ['God punish England'] 18 Februar 1915'. A similar medal shows Neptune with his trident and shell before the white cliffs of Dover, and has the same date (the day on which the U-boat campaign started). At that time the Germans had thirty U-boats, but by 1917 they had 300, which managed to sink between thirty and sixty ships a week early in that year, settling down to an average of fifteen a week as the year went on. Lloyd George's

Page 205, The Twentieth Century (I)
(1)Tom Thumb, 1906; (2) National Aerial Campaign, 1912; (3) *Lusitania*,
1915; (4) German submarine attack, 1915; (5) German air attack on
London, 1915 (photographed by the Imperial War Museum).

solution was the convoy system, and the use of Q-boats ('Mystery' or 'Hush' boats)—disguised as merchant craft, with one crew to act a 'panic' scene when a U-boat was sighted, and a fighting crew to shoot it up when it approached close enough. They accounted for 100–200 U-boats.

Goetz's most famous iron medal was the *Lusitania* medal, whose obverse depicted the ticket office of the Cunard Company in New York, with the figure of Death issuing tickets to a crowd of passengers, one of whom is reading a newspaper inscribed 'Submarine danger', while Count Bernstorff, the German ambassador in the USA, is raising a warning finger; the inscription reads, 'Business first'. On the reverse the *Lusitania*, with aeroplanes and guns on her deck, is seen sinking, her upturned bow looking like that of a warship. The inscription translates 'No contraband; the liner *Lusitania* sunk by a German submarine, 5 May 1915'.

The *Lusitania* was launched in 1906, and in 1907 crossed the Atlantic in the record time of 4 days 18 hr and 40 min. She was torpedoed 10 miles off Old Head of Kinsale, south-west Ireland on Friday, 7 (not 5) May 1915. On board was a crew of 600 and 1,250 passengers, including 179 Americans; her cargo consisted of copper, brass, furs and small-arms cartridges, but no guns or shells, and she was unarmed. The British government had warned the captain to look out for torpedoes and at 2.15 pm a torpedo was sighted; nothing could be done to avoid it and the ship sank in ten minutes with the loss of 1,198 lives. The event brought the USA into the war in 1917. The British government reversed the effect of the medal's propaganda by issuing copies for charity purposes. These have 'May' instead of the German medal's 'Mai', and they are quite common today.

Ludwig Gies issued an iron medal denouncing American aid to the Allies. Against a background of New York skyscrapers lies a raft in the river, laden with guns, its prow consisting of a monstrous head with donkey's ears, wearing a top hat decorated with stars and its open jaws full of dollars; it is inscribed '1914 1915'. The reverse is plain.

An iron medal by F. Eue (or Eve) recorded an air-raid on London in 1915. Its obverse has the bust of Count Zeppelin, and the reverse shows Tower Bridge and searchlights playing on two zeppelins that are bombing London. The inscription translates 'Air attack on London, 17,18. 8. 1915'. The official German report on the attack reads:

> On the night of 17–18 August our naval airships again attacked London. The City of London and important works along the Thames were freely bombed and good results observed. Factories and blast-furnaces at Woodbridge and Ipswich were also successfully bombed. In spite of heavy firing the airships were in no way damaged and all returned to their bases.

According to the British report the raid was carried out by zeppelins L 10, L 11 and L 14. L 14 returned after approaching the Norfolk coast and dropping its bombs into the sea, and L 11 crossed the coast at Herne Bay, cruised over part of Kent, dropped a few bombs in open fields and then returned. L 10, however, dropped bombs at Walthamstow and Leyton, doing considerable damage to houses at Leyton, which was the nearest any of the airships got to London; on its return route the L 10 dropped two bombs at Chelmsford without doing any damage. Count von Zeppelin was born in 1858 and his plans for a rigid airship date from 1873. He died in 1917.

The Dardanelles Expedition was the subject of both English and German medals. The English medal was cast in bronze by E. Carter Preston from designs by H. Tyson-Smith. The obverse shows the *River Clyde* at V Beach, with launches lying alongside her and troops landing under fire. On the reverse are four roundels containing a lion (Britain) a kangaroo (Australia), a kiwi (New Zealand) and a cock (France); in the middle is an anchor in a crowned wreath (the Navy); and in the angles, regimental badges of the West Riding Regiment, the Royal Dublin Fusiliers, the Royal Munsters and the Hampshires. In two circles are the names of the winners of the Victoria Cross. The British and French forces landed on 25 April 1915, and the landing at V Beach was made from the *River Clyde*, which was run ashore at that spot. Goetz cast a bronze medal, 2in across, to mark the failure of the Dardanelles Expedition. It shows a large Highlander advancing and carrying a small steamship with one funnel and two masts rigged with triangular sails, while at his feet a French infantryman is kneeling and firing; the inscription reads 'The sleep-walkers on Gallipoli'. The reverse shows two skeletons lying before wire entanglements, while above there is a star and a crescent moon and the dates 1915 and 1916. The evacuation was completed on 8 January 1916 with one casualty.

The battle of Jutland, fought between 31 May and 1 June 1916, was the subject of a competition organised by Sir Arthur Evans, President of the Royal Numismatic Society, to commemorate the battle and at the same time encourage a revival of die-cutting by hand instead of by machinery. The winning medal was struck in bronze from hand-cut dies by Harold Stabler, assisted by R. J. Richardson. Its obverse shows a British battleship firing at German ships on the horizon. The reverse has an anchor and two wreaths containing the names Jellicoe and Beatty. Jellicoe was in command, a strong leader with a brilliant brain, while Beatty was his second in command, a flamboyant aggressive man of action. Spink & Son issued a medal to commemorate those who died in the battle. The obverse has the White Ensign and the Union Jack crossed, with a trident between them and a small shield in front bearing the date 31 May 1916. An inscription round the perimeter reads 'To the glorious memory of those who fell that day'. The reverse has a wreath of oak leaves and the inscription 'May 31 1916. The German fleet attacked off the coast of Jutland and driven back into port with heavy loss. Admiral Sir John Jellicoe, commander in chief, Vice Admiral Sir David Beatty commanding battle cruiser fleet. Spink & Son 1916'.

David Lloyd George, the Prime Minister, was the subject of a medal issued in 1917, which shows him full face on the obverse, with the inscription 'David Lloyd George MCMXVII'. The reverse shows Britannia in an unusual pose, facing the viewer, holding a sword and a round shield; the inscription reads 'Victoria per laborem' ('Victory by toil'). The German medals of 1916, 1917 and 1918 stress the shortage of food and the fact that they are in retreat; they show the distress felt by the people of Germany, in sharp contrast to the arrogant propaganda medals with which they had begun the war.

J. R. Gaunt produced a victory medal in copper and gilt. The obverse shows Britannia holding a dove and a branch, while at her feet lies her helmet and, nearby, the head of her trident labelled 'Peace'; the inscription names the victorious countries. The reverse depicts a reclining lion, a child playing and a sword and shield lying nearby, with the inscription 'The Great War peace proclaimed June 1919'. Spink's produced a copper medal with the king's bust on the obverse, and the figure of Peace standing with a wreath on the reverse. When the Loughborough War Memorial Carillon Tower was built in 1923, a copper medal was struck, depicting the tower on the obverse, with a plain reverse. The tower, 87 ft tall, houses forty-seven bells in four chromatic octaves. The heaviest bell, weighing 4 tons 4 cwt, was presented by E. D. Taylor, head of the famous Loughborough bell-foundry.

WORLD WAR II

When war threatened again, medals were struck to mark Neville Chamberlain's flight to Munich in 1938. Leslie Pinches' design shows the head and shoulders of Chamberlain on the obverse, and, on the reverse, a spray of laurel with the words 'Out of this nettle danger he picked the flower safety'. Miss Muriel Hiley produced a bronze medal with the bust of Chamberlain on the obverse and a plain reverse.

World War II, unlike its predecessor, produced few medals. Miss Hiley's bronze medal bearing the bust of General Sir Archibald Wavell was one, and another medal was produced by Pinches for Garrard & Company, partially in aid of the Royal Air Force Benevolent Society. The obverse shows St Paul's Cathedral lit up by flashes all over the sky, and is inscribed 'Battle of London Sept. 1940, 1941, May'. The reverse shows the Tower of London from the river, with a flying-bomb overhead and a confusion of aerial 'dogfights', and the inscription 'Battle of London, June 1944, August'. Several thousand copies were struck in brass with a silver plated finish.

The Eighth Army's advance in 1943 was commemorated by two small medals struck in copper with suspension loops. The first has a view of Mount Vesuvius and the Bay of Naples with two sailing ships and the inscription '8th Army' on the obverse, and on the reverse, 'Commemorative medal of the entrance of the Allied Armies in Naples, 1 Oct 1943'. The second medal has a similar obverse, without the two sailing ships, and a reverse which reads, 'Commemorative medal of the entrance of the British Army in Italy, 10 July 1943'.

Page 210, The Twentieth Century (II)
(1) Edward VIII crowned, 1937; (2) M6 Motorway, 1969; (3) and (4)
St Paul's and the Tower of London under attack, 1940–44.

A reminder of World War II is to be found on the medals mourning the death of Sir Winston Churchill in 1965. Spink's medal has the bust of Churchill on the obverse, with his books and paintbrushes on a shelf behind him, and, on the reverse, the fully equipped figure of a soldier shaking his fist at planes flying over a raging sea towards him, with the words, 'Very well, alone'. Five hundred $2\frac{1}{4}$ in gold versions were sold for £100 each and one thousand $1\frac{1}{2}$ in for £35 each, while a large number of silver ones were also marketed. Hearn's medal has the head of Churchill on the obverse, and a pilot running to his Spitfire on the reverse, with the inscription 'Not so easily shall the lights of freedom die, 1940'; 1,000 gold medals were struck at £40 each and 5,000 silver at £2 10s 0d.

DOMESTIC AFFAIRS

There are not many twentieth-century medals connected with transport, though a few are interesting. In 1912 Vaughton's of Birmingham produced a copper medal showing a monoplane flying through the clouds above a church, with a biplane in the distance, on the obverse, and the inscription '1912 National Aerial Campaign Britain's future is in the air', on the reverse. This campaign remains something of a mystery today. The Aerial League of the British Empire evidently tried to raise £50,000 by 1 million shilling subscriptions in that year.

The launching of the *Queen Mary* was marked by a medal struck by the Royal Mint, which has the *Queen* steaming ahead on the obverse, and, on the reverse, a view through an arch, decorated with three coats of arms, of the skyscrapers of New York, and the inscription '*Queen Mary* commissioned 1936'. In 1967 Sir Francis Chichester's round the world voyage was the subject of a number of medals. Leslie Pinches designed a medal with a portrait of Sir Francis on the obverse, and *Gipsy Moth IV* against the background of a globe on the reverse, with the inscription '*Gipsy Moth IV*, World Voyage, 28.8.1966. 28.5.1967'. Platinum versions sold for £410, gold for £125 and silver for £6 15s 0d. Caroline Magrath designed a very similar medal, but with the inscription 'Single handed round the world, 1966–1967', on the reverse.

In 1971 the Nautical Medallion Society issued a medal in gold (£135) and silver (£8.75) designed by Richard Grasby and struck

Sir Francis Chichester and *Gipsy Moth IV*, 1967.

by Johnson Matthey & Co to mark the launching of the brig *T S Royalist* at Cowes. The obverse depicts the brig in full sail, while the reverse is inscribed '*T S Royalist* Sea Cadet Corps Training Brig named by Princess Anne 3 VIII 71'. The brig, the first fully square-rigged ship to be built since 1906, is two-masted, 76 ft long and capable of 12 knots under her 6,423 square feet of sail. The square rigging was chosen as being the most suitable for the teaching of seamanship. Training courses for twenty-six cadets at a time last a week, so that a thousand cadets a year will handle her. The medal is the first to be struck by the recently formed Nautical Medallion Society, which intends to produce five medals a year.

Motorways appeared on medals in 1969 when Vaughton's struck a bronze medal for the Black Country Society to mark the arrival of the M6 at Wednesbury. The obverse shows a motorway flyover running beside an electric railway, both heading towards an industrial area, while the reverse has a map marking the route of the 1769 canal linking Wednesbury with Birmingham.

The motor car and its driver were commemorated in a rather different way in 1970 with the issuing of 5,000 Jim Clark medals designed by Michael Rizzello for Alec Brook Ltd. On the obverse is a portrait of Clark, and on the reverse the Lotus Ford car No 82 in which he won the Indianapolis 500 Race, with the globe in the background surmounted by the Scottish lion.

Exhibitions and exhibitionists have found their place on commemorative medals in this century as in the last. A common medal to be found today is the copper medal depicting the 'Gigantic Wheel, Earl's Court, 1901', on the obverse, and the following inscription on the reverse: 'The Gigantic Wheel at Earl's Court is 284 feet in diameter & weighs about 900 tons. There are 40 cars, each to carry 30 persons. From the top of the wheel about 300 feet Windsor Castle is visible on the west'. In 1906 a white-metal medal was struck depicting a figure with a large head, dressed in a morning suit and standing on a table, with his hand on a pile of three books, and a bottle, glass, egg-cup, inkstand and quill nearby, together with the inscription 'Charles S Stratton known as Genl. Tom Thumb, 25 in high. Allen & Moore'. The reverse shows a four-pony stagecoach, with coachman and guard, and is inscribed, 'General Tom Thumb's equipage. Whole height 40 in body, 20 in by 11 in, ponies 28 in, crest, rising sun, arms Britannia and Liberty, supporters lion and eagle, motto "Go-a-head". Pub. by T. Barnem'.

In 1908 the Olympic Games were held in London, and the event was marked by a medal struck in gilt and white metal. On the obverse is a nude youth standing beneath a wreath held by two barely draped females; it is inscribed 'Olympic Games, London, 1908'. The reverse has a nude rider with helmet and shield galloping over a dragon and watched by a winged angel.

In 1924 the British Empire Exhibition was held on a 220-acre site in Wembley Park and George V's opening speech was relayed on the wireless. A number of medals were struck to mark the event. Macmillan's copper medal has a head with winged helmet on the obverse, with the inscription 'Commerce and Industry', and, on the reverse, a crane unloading a ship, with the inscription 'The British Empire Exhibition 1924'. P. Metcalfe produced a medal showing a power-plant on the obverse, and a lioness's head on the reverse, with the words 'Struck at the British Empire Exhibition 1924'.

Notes For Collectors
of Commemorative Medals

Because the collecting of commemorative medals is a comparatively new pursuit, no publisher has yet produced a handy catalogue listing current prices. The production of such a priced catalogue is dependent upon the complete classification of all commemorative medals. Definitive classifications of coins and medals are usually the work of nineteenth-century devotees, and, unfortunately, E. Hawkins got no further than 1760 with his research work (see Bibliography), and the period from 1760 to the 1930s has only been partly covered, though the majority of medals have been listed by M. H. Grant. Work is proceeding on a proper catalogue to cover the period after 1760, but it will be some time before it is finished. The collector who wants to known the market value of commemorative medals is forced to rely on sales lists periodically produced by the leading coin and medal dealers, which naturally only refer to the medals they happen to have in stock at the time of publication. This in turn means that there can be no definitely acceptable price put on a vast range of commemorative medals, and the collector may well strike a good bargain with those coin dealers who merely keep their commemorative medals in an old cardboard box.

Haphazard collecting can be rewarding, but with so vast a field before him the collector would be well advised to specialise. Coronation medals are an obvious example, and this category could be broadened to include any medal connected with royalty. Commemorative medals dealing with war can provide excellent pictorial scenes of battles, and many famous commanders are medallically portrayed. Propaganda war medals are particularly interesting.

Personalities in history is another line offering many subsections—for example, politicians (official and satirical medals), reformers, musicians, academics and villains. Events such as murders, marriages and memorials offer further lines for collection. Architectural and engineering achievements provide splendid pictorial medals, as do those connected with transport. A totally different approach for a would-be collector might be to build his collection on a geographical basis, say a county, whose events might be of national importance, or might just be connected with a parish church, a local society, a school or an athletic competition. One need not define commemorative medals as strictly as I have done in this book. Religious commemorative medals could cover those connected with events of national importance, with building or reconstructing churches, missionaries and temperance societies. Academic prize medals could cover those issued in schools to Nobel Gold Medals! Athletic medals cover most types of sport. Those issued by societies of various kinds are rewarding, too, and could take in medals issued at agricultural shows, or by photographic or stamp societies.

If a collector can accept what I have termed 'retrospective' medals as truly 'commemorative', then a whole world opens up to him at commercial prices. Odd medals and sets of medals struck today to commemorate events in the past have a ready sale. In 1964 M. & F. Feuchtwanger started a boom with their composers' set (Mozart, Schubert and Strauss). America has now become the foremost country in the production of retrospective medals and the National Commemorative Society there has provided opportunities for good-class collections. The Britannia Commemorative Society was started in 1966 for Great Britain, and it carries out a regular ballot of its members as to which historical subjects they would like commemorated. Such a ballot led to the striking of a medal to celebrate the 900th anniversary of William the Conqueror's coronation. Slade Hampton & Son of London produce historical series, beginning with one entitled 'Great Military Commanders' in 1970. This set includes Drake, Marlborough, Nelson, Wellington and Montgomery. The firm sells sets on the instalment plan, which enables collectors to see their collections growing regularly. Individual medals and sets struck today by various companies are always advertised in coin magazines and often in the national press.

Museums with Collections of Commemorative Medals

Many museums have small collections, but to list these would be impracticable. Museums often have the bulk of their collections in store, and it is advisable to warn them of your visit in advance. Some need at least two weeks' notice.

Bedfordshire	Bedford Museum
Berkshire	Reading Museum
Cambridgeshire	Fitzwilliam Museum, Cambridge
Derbyshire	Derby Museum
Dorset	Dorchester Museum
Gloucestershire	Bristol Museum
	City and Folk Museums, Gloucester
Hampshire	Winchester Museum
Herefordshire	Hereford Museum
Kent	Tunbridge Wells Museum
Lancashire	Blackburn Museum
	Liverpool Museum
	Manchester University Museum
Leicestershire	Newarke Museum, Leicester
Lincolnshire	City and County Museum, Lincoln
London	British Museum, Coin Room
	Guildhall Museum
	Imperial War Museum
	National Maritime Museum
	Victoria and Albert Museum
Oxfordshire	Ashmolean Museum, Oxford
Scotland	National Museum of Antiquities, Edinburgh
	Royal Scottish Museum, Edinburgh

Shropshire	Castle Gate Museum, Shrewsbury
Somerset	County Museum, Taunton
Warwickshire	Birmingham Museum
Wiltshire	Salisbury Museum
Yorkshire	Leeds Museum
	Sheffield Museum
	Yorkshire Museum, York

Bibliography

CATALOGUES

Grant, M. H. *Catalogue of British Medals since 1760;* originally published in the *British Numismatic Journal*, volumes 22 and 23 for years 1936–41. This catalogue simply gives a list of existing medals and in some cases indicates who issued them. At present it is the only catalogue dealing with the post-1760 period, though a full catalogue is in preparation and will be published in a few years.

Hawkins, E. *Medallic Illustrations of the History of Great Britain and Ireland*, 2 volumes (1885, reprinted by Spink & Son, 1969). This catalogue contains detailed descriptions of all medals struck between 1485 and 1760, some of which are illustrated. A few museums and libraries have folio volumes of illustrations for the medals described in this catalogue.

Pinkerton, J. *Medallic History of England to the Revolution of 1688* (1790). This catalogue gives general descriptions and numerous illustrations of the medals up to 1688.

EXHIBITION CATALOGUES

Guide to the Exhibition of English Medals in the British Museum (1891)
Guide to the Exhibition of Historical Medals in the British Museum (1924)

These two catalogues, published for special exhibitions, are invaluable pocket-size illustrated reference books.

REFERENCE BOOKS

Amstell, M. *A Start to Collecting Commemorative Medals* (1970)
Baker, W. S. *Medallic Portraits of Washington* (1965)

Bibliography

Beaulah, G. K. 'Medals of the Art Union of London', *British Numismatical Journal*, 36 (1967)

Belden, B. L. *Indian Peace Medals issued in the United States* (1927, 1959)

Betts, W. C. *American Colonial History Illustrated by Contemporary Medals* (1965 reprint)

Brown, M. D. *Catalogue of Medals Relating to the History of Transport* (1968)

Cochran, P. R. W. *Catalogue of the Medals of Scotland* (1884)

Conder, J. *Arrangement of Provincial Coins, Tokens and Medalets* (1798)

Cresswell, O. D. *Irish Medals* (1961)

Evelyn, J. *Discourse of Medals Antient and Modern* (1697)

Forrer, L. *Biographical Dictionary of Medalists*, 8 volumes (1904)

Freeman, S. E. *Medals relating to Medicine and Allied Sciences* (1964)

Greuber, H. A. 'Personal medals in alphabetical order, A-H', *Numismatical Chronicle* (1887–92)

Grinsell, L. V. *A Brief Numismatic History of Bristol* (1962)

Hill, G. F. *The Commemorative Medal in the Service of Germany* (1917)

Jamieson, M. A. *Medals Awarded to the North American Indian Chiefs, 1714–1922* (1936, reprinted 1961)

Loubat, J. F. *The Medallic History of the United States of America 1776–1876* (1878, reprinted 1967)

Mackay, J. *Commemorative Medals* (1970)

Poulson, N. *The White Ribbon*—medallic record of polar exploration 1818–1966 (1969)

Ruby, W. A. *Commemorative Coins of the United States* (1961)

Sandham, A. *Coins, Tokens and Medals of Dominion of Canada* (1869)

Slabaugh, A. R. *United States Commemorative Coinage* (1963)

Snelling, T. *Thirty-nine Plates of English Medals* (1776)

Svarstad, C. *Medals of Actors, Singers and Dancers* (1963)

Taxay, D. *An Illustrated History of US Commemorative Coinage* (1967)

Thoyras, P. R. de. *Metallick History of Reigns of William III and Queen Mary, Queen Anne and King George I* (1747)

Welch, C. *Medals struck by Corporation of London, 1831–1893* (1894)

Weber, R. Parkes. *Medals and Medallions of Nineteenth Century Relating to England by Foreign Artists* (1894)

Wroth, W. 'Personal Medals', *Numismatical Chronicle* (1886)

Index